POWERFUL
Partnerships

A Handbook for
Principals Mentoring
Assistant Principals

Gary Bloom | Martin L. Krovetz

CORWIN PRESS
A SAGE Company

For information:

Corwin Press
A SAGE Company
2455 Teller Road
Thousand Oaks, California 91320
www.corwinpress.com

SAGE India Pvt. Ltd.
B 1/I 1 Mohan Cooperative
   Industrial Area
Mathura Road, New Delhi 110 044
India

SAGE Ltd.
1 Oliver's Yard
55 City Road
London, EC1Y 1SP
United Kingdom

SAGE Asia-Pacific Pte. Ltd.
33 Pekin Street #02-01
Far East Square
Singapore 048763

Printed in the United States of America

Library of Congress Cataloging-in-Publication Data

Bloom, Gary, 1953–
  Powerful partnerships : a handbook for principals mentoring assistant principals / Gary Bloom, Martin L. Krovetz.
    p. cm.
  Includes bibliographical references and index.
  ISBN 978-1-4129-2770-3 (cloth)—ISBN 978-1-4129-2771-0 (pbk.)
  1. Assistant school principals—In-service training—Handbooks, manuals, etc.   2. School principals—Handbooks, manuals, etc.   3. School management and organization—Handbooks, manuals, etc.   4. Mentoring in education—Handbooks, manuals, etc.   I. Krovetz, Martin L. II. Title.

LB1738.5.B56 2009
371.2'012—dc22   2008028633

This book is printed on acid-free paper.

08 09 10 11 12   10 9 8 7 6 5 4 3 2 1

Acquisitions Editor:	Dan Alpert
Associate Editor:	Megan Bedell
Production Editor:	Appingo Publishing Services
Cover Designer:	Rose Storey
Graphic Designer:	Karine Hovsepian

CONTENTS

ABOUT THE AUTHORS

Gary Bloom is the lead author of *Powerful Partnerships: A Mentoring Handbook for Principals and Their Assistants.* He currently serves as Associate Director of the New Teacher Center at the University of California, Santa Cruz (http://www.newteachercenter.org). Gary has served as a bilingual teacher, principal, director of curriculum, and assistant superintendent for human resources. He served as the superintendent of the Aromas-San Juan Unified School District, known for its innovative programs such as graduation exhibitions, a teacher-led high school, and teacher peer review. Gary is a Kellogg National Fellow, former adjunct faculty to San Jose State University's Educational Administration graduate program, and has consulted and presented on a variety of topics throughout the United States, Canada, the United Kingdom, and Latin America. Currently, he is supporting a number of urban school districts and states in designing and implementing coaching-based leadership induction programs, and in increasing the capacity of principals to serve as instructional leaders. He has published articles in ASCD, AASA and ACSA's educational leadership journals, most recently on the topics of teacher leadership, professional learning communities, new teacher support, principal induction, teacher supervision, and the appropriate use of technology. He is lead author of *Blended Coaching: Skills and Strategies for Principal Development*, Corwin Press, 2005, and co-editor of *The Peer Assistance and Review Reader*, 2000. He can be reached at gsbloom@gmail.com.

Martin L. Krovetz, PhD, is Director of the Leading for Equity and Achievement Design Center (LEAD; http://www.lead-ces.com), a regional center of the Coalition of Essential Schools. From 1991–2006 he was a professor of Educational Leadership at San Jose State University. During that time he developed and coordinated the Master's in Collaborative Leadership Program. From 1977–1991 he was a high school principal in

Santa Cruz, California. He is the author of *Fostering Resilience: Expecting All Students to Use Their Minds and Hearts Well* (1999, 2008), and he is coauthor, with Gilberto Arriaza, of *Collaborative Teacher Leadership: How Teachers Can Foster Equitable Schools* (2006), published by Corwin Press. He has published in numerous journals and presents at national conferences, including ASCD and the Coalition of Essential Schools. He received his PhD in social psychology from the University of North Carolina and BA from the University of Florida. He can be reached at marty@krovetz.net.

ACKNOWLEDGMENTS

This book reflects knowledge and insights we have gained in working with hundreds of respected colleagues in schools around the country. The individuals who have contributed to this book are too numerous to name. We dedicate this book to the many thousands of educators who successfully take on the challenges of school leadership out of a commitment to students and to social justice.

We thank our colleagues at the New Teacher Center at the University of California, Santa Cruz, and the College of Education at San Jose State University, who have helped us to refine many of the ideas that are presented here. We also thank Dan Alpert and his colleagues at Corwin Press for their help in bringing this book to life.

Gary dedicates the book to his daughter, Ariel Stonebloom, a third-generation teacher who some day might be just crazy enough to be an extraordinary principal.

PUBLISHER'S ACKNOWLEDGMENTS

Corwin Press gratefully acknowledges the contributions of the following reviewers:

Dawnel Sonntag, Principal
Monroe Middle School, San Jose, CA

Lori King, Principal
Washington Open, Santa Clara, CA

Roxanne Cardona, Principal
Elementary Public School, Bronx, NY

INTRODUCTION

W e have written this book because we know how important principals and assistant principals are to schools, their students, and staff. We have seen how leaders and schools suffer when principal/assistant principal relationships are neglected or are overwhelmed by day-to-day demands. We have seen too many assistant principals promoted into principalships without receiving the kind of mentoring and job experience that would have prepared them for their challenging new positions.

Both of us have served as principals and assistant principals and have taught and coached principals and their assistants, as individuals and as teams, for many years. This accumulated experience has taught us that school leadership is not for the faint of heart. You have to be willing to take risks and to tell it like it is, particularly in working with your closest colleagues. You have to be willing to bring structure and discipline to your daily work. The principal/assistant principal relationship is a key but often neglected component of your daily work.

Think of this as a workbook for your principal/assistant principal team. It is a book to read and work through together. It is meant to be a practical tool to help principal/assistant principal teams build and manage their relationships. It is meant to be a guide that will help you to grow as leaders and to have a more positive impact upon your students.

You probably spend more waking hours with your leadership colleagues than you do with your partners or spouses (that's assuming you have found the time to have and maintain personal relationships). But it is unlikely that your professional partnership was proceeded by any "prenuptial counseling," and there are no therapists out there waiting to patch up your relationship if you hit a rough spot. There haven't been (until now) any "self-help" books out there to help you build a successful relationship.

This isn't exactly a self-help book, and it certainly isn't a marriage manual. However, like books in that genre, it will require you to exercise some self-discipline if you are to take advantage of what it has to offer.

There are around 93,000 school principals in the United States, and a similar number of assistant principals. Over the past few years, the critical importance of school leadership to school improvement has been widely recognized. Also recognized is the growing shortage of qualified candidates for these leadership positions.

In their book *School Leadership That Works*, Marzano, Waters, and McNulty share the results of a meta-analysis of sixty-nine research studies that examine the impact of leadership on student achievement. They conclude that "school leadership has a substantial effect on student achievement," an effect second only to teacher quality. Your work has a direct impact upon kids.

High levels of turnover in the principalship and assistant principalship are a fact. A wave of baby boomer retirements is beginning to hit school districts hard. As a result, both principals and assistant principals are entering their jobs with less experience than they might have had in prior generations. The current median age of principals in this country is around 51, about three years higher than it was a decade ago; the retirement wave is just now approaching the shore. If you are a principal reading this book, odds are good that you have five or fewer years experience in your position and that you came into the principalship with just a few, if any, years of prior administrative experience. If you are an assistant principal, it is likely that you have ten or fewer years of teaching experience, and, if you are willing and able, you will be drafted into a principalship very soon. About 73 percent of current principals with five or less years of experience served as assistant principals before taking that seat where the buck stops.

The assistant principalship is a position that has received little attention. At the local level, APs are often relegated to spending their days handling student discipline and activities with little opportunity to exercise more sophisticated leadership. At the state and national level, there has been little said or done to address this group, people who are nonetheless key actors in our nation's schools, and who are the next generation of school principals.

What we have attempted to create here is a toolkit that will both strengthen your school leadership team and prepare the assistant principal to assume a principalship. We suggest that you each have a copy of the book (doubles our sales—we're no dummies) and that you work through it together.

Using this book effectively won't be easy. We are asking you to bring some structure and discipline to your relationship while you keep the lid on jobs where you are deluged by demands and seldom have the time to slow down and think. This brings to mind one of the great paradoxes of leadership; you must slow down and think strategically together in order to create the systems and culture that will give you the time to slow down and think strategically together.

The book is organized into four major sections. In the first section, we focus on building a partnership between the principal and assistant principal. We provide you with tools to help you develop a shared vision for your relationship and your school, and for designing a plan for communication and professional development. In the second section, we focus on leadership as stewardship—the shared implementation of the critical management responsibilities that are the prerequisites of school improvement. In the third section, we deal with the fundamental leadership challenges that come with working with people, and in the fourth, we walk you through some of the most important instructional leadership responsibilities shared by principal/assistant principal teams.

We make frequent reference in this book to the Interstate School Leadership Licensure Consortium (ISLLC) Standards. These professional standards for school leaders have now been adapted and adopted in one form or another by most states as a framework for the preparation, evaluation, and ongoing professional development of school principals. We also refer frequently to the work of Robert Marzano and his colleagues at McREL, particularly their meta-analysis of the research on school leadership, through which they have identified twenty-one leadership behaviors that are correlated with increased school leadership. If readers are not already familiar with the ISLLC standards and McREL's *School Leadership That Works*, we suggest that they become so, and consider them companion pieces to this book.

HOW TO USE THIS BOOK

In each section of the book, we have outlined a variety of subtopics, and under each subtopic we have provided some brief *background, discussion questions, shared activities, activities for the AP (assistant principal)*, and *tools*. We suggest that you read each subtopic section as a team, and then spend a few minutes responding together to the *discussion questions*. You will find that these questions are simple and obvious, and probably raise issues that you have taken for granted in your work with one another. Review the *shared activities* and *activities for the AP*, and decide which of these you are going to take on. Some of the *tools* we have provided may help you with these tasks. Commit to these activities, and check in with one another on them during your regular meetings. For some topics we have provided *additional resources*, one or two select books or Web sites that we think are worth checking out for more information.

In this book we use the terms *partnership* and *leadership team*. You might be a team of two, a principal and one assistant; you might be a leadership team of eight, with multiple APs and leaders in other roles at the table. Interpret and use what we suggest as it best serves your configuration.

We suggest that you each read the entire first section of the book, *Building a Powerful Partnership*. Take the time to have all of the shared discussions we have suggested, and take on the *activities* that would seem to be of value to you. At a minimum, we urge you to engage in the self-assessment, goal setting, and planning activities, and that you commit to a meeting plan and to a deliberate distributed rotation of responsibilities for the assistant principal(s).

You may choose to be more selective as you work your way through Parts II through IV. We suggest that you review the contents, and, based upon your interests, self-assessments, and goals, build a plan and timeline to address those topics that would appear of most value to you. There may be more in this book than any principal/assistant principal team can do in a busy school year, and there are certainly many important areas for collaboration and professional growth that we have omitted. We hope that this book will help you to create a new, ongoing model for your relationship that extends beyond any one year. We encourage you to bring other topics and activities not addressed here to your relationship, and we ask you to share your ideas and feedback with us. If this book brings some focus to your partnership and accelerates your learning in a few key leadership areas, it will have served its purpose.

A NOTE TO CENTRAL OFFICE LEADERS

We anticipate that many central office leaders will recognize the needs we are trying to address here, and will purchase this book for their principals and assistants. This book and the process it describes can be useful to you as you build the capacity of your site leadership teams and grow your next generation of principals. If you choose to pursue this course, we have several recommendations for you.

• Make it very clear to your principals that one of their responsibilities is to grow their assistants into future principals. Address this responsibility in your principals' annual goals and through your district's principal supervision process.

• Make the principal/assistant principal relationship a focus of your leadership professional development. Give teams time to do this work at your management meetings, and structure opportunities for sharing across site teams at those meetings.

BUILDING A POWERFUL PARTNERSHIP

In Part I we lay the foundation for the creation of an effective leadership team, and for the establishment and maintenance of relationships within your team that will contribute to your professional growth and personal satisfaction, as well as have a positive impact upon student achievement at your site. We suggest that the assistant principalship should be viewed and managed as an apprenticeship for the principalship, and that one of the principal's most important responsibilities is to mentor his or her assistants. We argue that a leadership team must bring structure and discipline to its work if it is to meet its potential. We provide nuts and bolts tools for you use together in order to bring that structure and discipline to your team. We remind you that none of this will happen by accident. Think of this book as a set of lesson plans that will only have an impact if you use them; don't just read this book—act on it.

In his book *Good to Great*, Jim Collins (2001) shares the following research-based characteristics of successful leaders.

- They set up their successors for even greater success in the next generation.
- They are self-effacing and understated.
- They look out the window to attribute success to factors other than themselves. When things go poorly, however, they look in the mirror and blame themselves, taking full responsibility.
- They build a culture around the idea of freedom and responsibility within a framework.
- They fill that culture with self-disciplined people who are willing to go to extreme lengths to fulfill their responsibilities.

Let this vision of leadership shape the development of your team.

A COACHING-BASED RELATIONSHIP

The apprentice sushi master: His education seems a matter of passive observation. The young man cleans the dishes, mops the kitchen floor, bows to the clients, fetches ingredients, and in the meantime follows from the corners of his eyes, without ever asking a question, everything the sushi masters are doing. For no less than three years he watches them without being allowed to make actual sushi for the patrons of the restaurant-an extreme case of exposure without practice. He is waiting for the day on which he will be invited to make his own sushi, which he will do with remarkable dexterity.

—Frans De Waal, *The Ape and the Sushi Master*, 2001

A coach tells you what you don't want to hear so that you can see what you don't want to see so that you can be what you have always wanted to be.

—Tom Landry

To lead people, walk beside them . . . As for the best leaders, the people do not notice their existence. The next best, the people honor and praise. The next, the people fear; and the next, the people hate . . . When the best leader's work is done the people say, "We did it ourselves!"

—Lao-Tsu

Background

Just what is the job of the assistant principal? Is he or she there to, literally, assist the principal? Or is the AP an instructional leader in his or her own right? Is the AP's primary responsibility service to the principal, or to the school? From the principal's perspective, is the AP a helper or an associate? Should a principal grow his or her APs and delegate increasingly significant responsibilities to them, or focus AP energies on management tasks so that he or she can reign as the site instructional leader?

We suggest that effective principal/assistant principal relationships are grounded in the following assumptions and understandings.

- Principals and their assistants should work together as a collaborative team. That team serves the students' and school's best interests. The buck stops with the principal, but leadership and responsibility are shared, and debate and diversity of opinion are embraced.
- Principals have a responsibility to grow those around them. Effective leaders cultivate leadership in others, and effective principals recognize that one of their primary responsibilities is to ready their assistants to assume principalships.
- Strong learning organizations have coaching cultures. Effective principals use coaching, rather than bossing, to grow their people and manage their organizations. They build cultures where coaching and a learning community are norms.

Principals must not forget that they are role models for those around them. Primatologist Frans De Waal (2001) explores what it means to be human in his wonderful book *The Ape and the Sushi Master*. Among our many primate talents is the propensity to learn by imitation, or emulation.

De Waal tells the story of the Kellogg family, who brought an early halt to their experiment corearing their son, Donald, with a chimpanzee when Donald began to grunt rather than talk. It became apparent that Donald was more inclined to ape the ape, rather than vice versa.

Perhaps one of the reasons that school reform is so difficult is that we learn by imitation and that we learn the roles of teacher and principal in our youth when we are most impressionable. Most of us have caught ourselves thinking, "I am becoming my mother or father." Are we also becoming our teachers and principals and, in the process, replicating ineffective practice?

So, principal, yours is an awesome responsibility, as you model principal behaviors for those that follow in your footsteps. We add a note of caution to APs: Be mindful of your human tendency to imitate your leader; consciously determine those leadership behaviors you want to emulate, and those you want to avoid.

Principals also shape the next generation of school leadership through the schools that they help to create and through the supervision and coaching they provide their protégés.

We sometimes lose sight of the fact that those of us who do the work of schooling are professionals. We bring specialized knowledge to our work, and a commitment to meeting professional standards and continuing personal growth in our chosen field. The relationships we hope to build between supervisees and supervisors are different from the stereotypical boss/subordinate relationships we might expect to find in a fast food joint or in boot camp. Effective supervisors in a professional setting don't spend a lot of time giving orders; rather, they dedicate themselves to building the capacity and self-actualization of their supervisees.

At the foundation of a "learning organization" that builds individual capacity are what we call coaching relationships between supervisors and supervisees. Both of you, principal and assistant, supervise staff, and you want to nurture coaching relationships between yourselves and those you supervise. You also want to build a coaching relationship as the base of the apprenticeship you are building for the assistant principal. The coaching relationship that you build between each other can serve as a model for the rest of your staff and can be a powerful influence on the culture of your school.

Let's contrast a traditional boss/subordinate relationship between a principal and assistant principal with the coaching-based apprenticeship we are proposing:

Boss/Subordinate Relationship	Coaching-Based Apprenticeship
• Directive	• Collaborative
• Boss as teller and decision maker	• Boss as listener and facilitator
• Boss's success as goal	• Team success as goal
• Stable team as goal	• Dynamic team and succession pipeline as goal
• Task- and problem-driven	• Process driven

A coaching-based apprenticeship is more than a typical mentoring relationship. Mentoring relationships are informal and voluntary (and we all, no matter what our roles or career stages, should seek out mentors). A coaching-based apprenticeship is built upon firm commitments of collaboration and mutual support. It is embedded in a supervisory relationship but, as we have described above, it is about more than just "getting the job done."

The book *Blended Coaching: Skills and Strategies to Support Principal Development* (Bloom, et al., 2005) outlines a conceptual framework for professional coaching and helps readers develop and practice the basic skills exercised by leadership coaches. At the core of coaching conversations is language such as the following:

Sample Blended Coaching Language Stems

Paraphrasing
- So . . .
- Let me make sure I understand . . .
- In other words, . . .

Clarifying
- Could you tell me more about . . . ?
- Tell me what you mean by . . .
- Could you give me an example . . . ?
- How is that different from . . . ?

Interpretation
- What you are describing could mean . . .
- Could it be that what you are saying is . . . ?

Mediational
- What criteria do you use to . . . ?
- What might happen if . . . ?
- How would it look . . . ?
- What is the impact of . . . on students . . . ?
- How do you decide . . . ?

Instructional
- Can I describe some options for you . . . ?
- A couple of things to keep in mind are . . .
- Research seems to indicate . . .
- Sometimes it is helpful if . . .

Summarizing
- You have stated that your goal is . . .
- Let's review the key points in our discussion . . .
- Tell me your next steps . . .
- So this is your homework . . .

Transformational
- Let's try a role-play . . .
- Ground that assessment for me . . .
- Could you make a different assessment . . . ?
- How could we turn that rut story into a river story . . . ?
- What new "way of being" are you willing to try out . . . ?

Here are some examples to give you a taste of how a coaching-based relationship might sound in comparison to a traditional boss/subordinate relationship:

The AP's Problem/Need	Traditional Boss Response	Coaching-Based Response
Should I suspend Josh for fighting?	I would give him five days!	What do you think, given the circumstances and our rules and process?
I'm uncomfortable telling Ms. Jones that we are not going to rehire her next year.	Be brave, it will be OK, or I will do it for you if you like.	How do you want the meeting to go? Let's do a role-play.
The math department isn't implementing common assessments. I don't think we're getting anywhere with them.	I had the same problem with the English department, and solved it by bringing in the union rep.	Tell me what you have done so far. What could be your next steps?
I didn't get that report in to the federal programs office in time.	That is not good for us. Don't let it happen again!	That is not good for us. What can we do to ensure that this won't happen again?
The school board wants us to do a presentation on our Advanced Placement programs.	This is going to be very political. I'd better handle it.	Doing the presentation would be a good experience for you, but it is high-stakes. Let's plan this together and rehearse.

This book isn't a primer on coaching. We're going to assume that you understand the basics of coaching: listening, giving nonjudgmental feedback, asking open-ended questions, guiding the coachee through a reflective process that leads to the establishment of goals and action plans, and following up with the coachee to ensure that the actions are taken and that lessons are derived from the outcomes. But coaching doesn't come easily in the pressure cooker environment of school leadership. We suggest that you engage in the following exercises as a foundation for the balance of the work you might do together in taking advantage of this book.

Discussion Questions

- What supervisor/supervisee relationships have and haven't worked for each of you, and what have been the characteristics of these relationships?
- How would you characterize your principal/assistant principal relationship to date?
- What is your shared vision for your relationship, and what will it take to make that vision a reality?

Shared Activities

- Take turns practicing coaching one another. The coachee presents a problem or dilemma, and the coach facilitates the coachee in arriving

BOSS/SUBORDINATE RELATIONSHIP

Mike explained to his APs that he sees himself as the bus driver. They are all on the bus; he has the wheel, the throttle, and the brakes. The APs are passengers, but that does not mean they don't have responsibilities. If they see a hazard on the road or suspect that something is going wrong mechanically, it is their job to let Mike know. They also take the lead in making sure everybody else on the bus is behaving and has their needs met while Mike navigates the highways.

We don't think this is a particularly good model for the principal/AP relationship. An alternative might be the relationship between an airline captain and his or her first officer. On a commercial flight, the captain has final authority, but that doesn't mean that he or she is always operating the flight controls. On one leg of the flight, the captain might be responsible for take off and landing and the first officer for radios and navigation, and on the next leg those responsibilities might be reversed. The captain and first officer rotate duties and share responsibilities, but one of the captain's jobs is to monitor the first officer's performance, provide ongoing feedback, and prepare him or her to assume the role of pilot in command.

Other analogous relationships might be those between an orchestra conductor and first violin, between head chef and line chef, between center and forward. What analogous relationships would best portray your vision for your relationship?

---

at next steps in relation to the problem or dilemma by using the language stems outlined above. If there are more than two of you in your leadership team, use the *Problem-Posing/Problem-Solving Protocol* provided in the following Tools section.

- Copy the *Blended Coaching Language Stems* in the Tools section and put them somewhere conspicuous as you have coaching conversations. Make them "habits of mind."

Activities for the AP

- Invite the principal or another colleague to observe you meeting with a staff member (such as a supervisee) or a student in a coaching conversation. Have the observer use the *Observing Coaching Conversations* worksheet from the Tools section and provide you with feedback on your coaching behaviors.

Additional Resources

Bloom, G., Warren, B., Castagna, C., & Moir, E. (2005). *Blended coaching: Skills and strategies to support principal development.* Thousand Oaks, CA: Corwin Press.

Daresh, J. (2001). *Leaders helping leaders.* Thousand Oaks, CA: Corwin Press.

Tools

- Problem-Posing/Problem-Solving Protocol
- Observing Coaching Conversations
- Blended Coaching Language Stems

Problem-Posing/Problem-Solving Protocol

5 min. A shares a dilemma or issue while B and C listen.

2 min. B and C paraphrase what they've heard to be the key elements or issues and ask clarifying questions. A responds.

4 min. B and C have a speculative conversation with one another while A listens, taking notes but not speaking. They may
- summarize what they have heard;
- suggest interpretations of the situation;
- raise mediational questions they might ask of A; or
- speculate around possible courses of action.

4 min. Partners engage in three-way dialogue. B and C constrain their interaction to coaching language: paraphrasing, clarifying, summarizing, interpreting, asking mediational questions, summarizing, or suggesting transformational strategies.

Observing Coaching Conversations		
Blended Coaching Stems	**Coach's Language**	**Coachee Response**
Paraphrasing • So . . . • Let me make sure I understand . . . • In other words, . . .		
Clarifying Questions • Could you tell me more about . . . • Tell me what you mean by . . . ? • Could you give me an example . . . ? • How is that different from . . . ?		
Interpretation • What you are describing could mean . . . • Could it be that what you are saying is . . . ?		
Mediational Questions • What criteria do you use to . . . ? • What might happen if . . . ? • How would it look . . . ? • What is the impact of . . . on students . . . ?		
Summarizing • You have stated that your goal is . . . • Let's review the key points in our discussion . . . • Tell me your next steps . . . • So this is your homework . . .		
Transformational Coaching • Let's try a role play . . . • What new "way of being" are you willing to try out . . . ?		

Blended Coaching Language Stems

Paraphrasing
- So . . .
- Let me make sure I understand . . .
- In other words, . . . ?

Clarifying
- Could you tell me more about . . . ?
- Tell me what you mean by . . .
- Could you give me an example . . . ?
- How is that different from . . . ?

Interpretation
- What you are describing could mean . . .
- Could it be that what you are saying is . . . ?

Mediational
- What criteria do you use to . . . ?
- What might happen if . . . ?
- How would it look . . . ?
- What is the impact of . . . on students . . . ?
- How do you decide . . . ?

Instructional
- Can I describe some options for you . . . ?
- A couple of things to keep in mind are . . .
- Research seems to indicate . . .
- Sometimes it is helpful if . . .

Summarizing
- You have stated that your goal is . . .
- Let's review the key points in our discussion . . .
- Tell me your next steps . . .
- So this is your homework . . .

Transformational
- Let's try a role play . . .
- Ground that assessment for me . . .
- Could you make a different assessment . . . ?
- How could we turn that rut story into a river story . . . ?
- What new "way of being" are you willing to try out . . . ?

BUILDING AND COMMUNICATING
A SHARED VISION

You've got to be very careful if you don't know where you're going, because you might not get there.

—Yogi Berra

Background

Before we go too far down the road on this project of building the strength of your partnership, we should stop and ask, "Are you really heading in the same direction?" If you are like most school leadership teams, your aspirations are fairly well aligned around a school plan and around commitments like "closing the achievement gap." And, if you are like most teams around the country, each of you will have a different vision and priorities when pressed to provide more detail.

Consistent across the research on leadership is the finding that effective leaders are explicit, consistent, and relentless in building, communicating, and implementing a shared vision. McREL's twenty-one proven school leadership behaviors can all be linked to a leader's promotion of a school's vision, and at least four of them speak directly to the topic: fostering shared beliefs, establishing and communicating clear goals, inspiring and leading innovations, and communicating and operating from strong beliefs about schooling.

Few leadership ideas are more poorly understood or implemented than those regarding vision. Many principals' visions and their schools' mission statements don't go beyond heady "mom and apple pie" rhetoric like "all kids can learn" or "we provide a world-class education." Powerful visions are concrete, specific, and achievable. They are embodied in statements like "all of our students will graduate meeting four-year college entry requirements" and "our decisions will be made based on what is best for our students, not on the basis of what is most convenient for our adults."

A clear, shared vision is at the foundation of a strong principal/assistant principal relationship, and we urge you to take the time to develop a deep, shared understanding of your aspirations for your school.

If you have not already done so, it may be a valuable exercise for you to work with your staff and community to develop a written statement of vision, values, and mission. Such statements should reflect dynamic interaction between the school's leaders, staff, and community. In the process, remember that there is nothing emptier than a vision statement that cannot be evidenced through the behavior of the adults and students at a school or measured in a concrete way.

Discussion Questions

- Do you have a clear, shared vision for your school? What is it?
- What evidence can you identify around your school that demonstrates your vision is more than rhetoric?
- What are the most significant barriers that stand in the way of achieving your vision?

Shared Activities

- Independently write statements describing your vision for your school. Compare and discuss.
- Interview students, staff, and parents. Can they describe a common or personal vision for the school?
- Discuss the *Vision-Driven Questions* included in the Tools section.
- An "elevator speech" is a short description of your school, what makes it unique, your vision for the school, your key strategies for improvement—basically, a speech you can make between the first and twentieth floors. Develop your "elevator speeches" and practice them together. Ultimately, everyone on your staff should be able to give a similar rap.
- Develop a plan that outlines a limited number of actions/activities that your leadership team can engage in to build consensus around and knowledge of your shared vision for your school.

Activities for the AP

- Research model vision statements and bring examples to your leadership team.
- Use the *Decision Analysis Matrix* to review decisions you have made recently at your school. Share your findings with your leadership team.

Additional Resources

Peterson, K. (1995). *Building a collective vision.* Naperville, IL: North Central Regional Educational Laboratory. Retrieved August 17, 2008, from http://www.ncrel.org/sdrs/areas/issues/educatrs/leadrshp/le100.htm

Tools

- Vision-Driven Questions
- Decision Analysis Matrix

Vision-Driven Questions

Big Picture

- What are the three most important measurable outcomes we hope to produce in this school?
- What would we hope an outsider would notice first when visiting our school's classrooms?
- How do we want students and staff to experience our school on a daily basis?
- Ten years from now, what will be in place here as evidence of our leadership?

Our People

- How do race, ethnicity, gender, and social class play into our programs, school culture, and their outcomes?
- What is our relationship with our parents and community?
- To what degree is teaching practice here private or public?
- How do teachers exercise leadership? How is student voice part of our culture and decision making?
- How are classified staff members integrated into our team?
- What motivates our staff and students?

Our Organization

- What does it mean to be a professional here? How high and consistent are our standards for adults?
- What are the relative roles and importance of our sports, academic, and vocational programs?
- What is the role of department chairs?
- How are special education students included in our programs, and how do we ensure that their needs are met?
- How do we meet the needs of English language learners and other special populations?

Decision Analysis Matrix

What was the decision?	Who was involved in the process?	Who made it?	Who will be impacted?	What interests were served by the decision?	What resources were used in making and implementing the decision?	How does the decision support your vision and mission?

YOU NEED TO MEET

*If you had to identify, in one word, the reason why the human race has not
achieved, and never will achieve, its full potential, that word would be "meetings."*
—Dave Barry, *Things That It Took Me 50 Years to Learn*

Background

We're going to make a prediction. Despite your best intentions to implement a deliberate coaching-based apprentice relationship, and to have a well-coordinated leadership team grounded in solid communication, you are going to stumble. You will not meet as often as you need to. When you do meet, you will spend your time dealing with short-term problems and logistics and never get to coaching conversations and strategic issues.

If your leadership team is to achieve its potential, you are going to have to invest time in the relationship, and to exercise discipline in your use of that time. You should recognize that there are different types of meetings, and that effective meetings are governed by norms. Here are ways to organize your meeting times.

- Daily "stand-up" tactical meetings to brief one another and plan for the day (e.g., 7:30-7:45 a.m. in the principal's office)
- Weekly tactical meetings to track larger issues and progress on strategic initiatives (e.g., 7:30-9:00 a.m. every Tuesday in the principal's office)
- Monthly strategic meetings only for the purpose of reviewing major strategic issues (e.g., 3:30-5:30 p.m. every fourth Tuesday, off site)
- Bi-weekly one-on-one principal/assistant meetings focused on the topics and activities outlined in this book (e.g., every other Tuesday from 9:00-9:45 a.m.)

As hard as it may be, you really do have to commit to this sort of schedule and process if you are to be an effective team. And, you have to be willing to insist that your meetings be conducted efficiently. A first step in conducting efficient meetings is to collaboratively develop a set of norms. It may seem odd to develop written norms for a small group of intimate colleagues. ("Why have norms? We see each other all the time and things are going fine!") The thing is, you have norms whether they are explicit and written or not. For example, the unwritten norm with one high school leadership team we know is never to meet when a meeting is scheduled, only when summoned by the principal. The norm is to have no agenda and to revisit items meeting after meeting because no one follows through on any decisions that might be made. These are the norms, everybody complies with them, everyone is frustrated, and no one says a thing.

Most groups that take the time to develop explicit norms come up with some common statements: start on time, work from an agenda, value each other's perspectives, etc. Developing norms is easy; sticking to them takes real dedication.

A WORD ON INTERRUPTIONS

School leaders make hundreds of decisions every day, and engage in many hundreds of interactions. Unlike most other workers, who are responsible for a narrower range of tasks in a more defined work space, administrators are up and about and at the beck and call of students, parents, the district, and staff. They literally become addicted to interruption and distraction, unable to sustain focus on any one thing for more than a few minutes. Technology exacerbates this pattern, as e-mail, blackberries, and walkie-talkie earpieces intrude on every conversation. An over-implemented desire to provide an open door, service-oriented office can contribute to the problem. When it is time for your team meetings, turn off the technology, tell your secretary to hold the calls and interruptions unless the building is on fire, and close the door.

Discussion Questions

- What has been working for you, and what hasn't, in relation to your meeting schedule and meeting conduct?

Shared Activities

- Agree on a meeting plan and schedule and get it in your calendars. Complete the *Meetings Worksheet* provided.
- Develop written norms for your meetings and your relationship.
- Create a table to record your meeting times, topics and outcomes. For a month, record your pattern of meetings, and then have a discussion to review your findings.

Activities for the AP

- Develop and implement meeting norms and a meeting plan with a group that you are responsible for.

Additional Resources

Lencioni, P. (2004). *Death by meeting*. San Francisco: Jossey-Bass.

Tools

- Meetings Worksheet
- Leadership Team Meeting Notes

Meetings Worksheet

Our Shared Commitments Around Meeting and Communication

As a school leadership team, we recognize that the quality of our communication and collaboration will have an impact upon our staff and students and must be of the highest priority. While we strive to build strong personal and informal relationships, we also recognize the importance of making formal and explicit agreements with one another, and standing by them.

Our Meeting and Communication Norms

-
-
-
-

Our Meeting Plan

Type	Purpose	Frequency	When and Where
Daily stand up	Tactical updates on immediate concerns, day's events, and plans	Daily	
Weekly tactical	Review progress on strategic concerns and initiatives, delegate responsibilities, weekly planning	Weekly	
Monthly strategic	Review data and other outcomes, plan major initiatives, focus on the big picture	Monthly	
Monthly 1:1	Focus on principal/assistant relationship and individual personal and professional growth	Bi-weekly	

Sample Administrative Team Meeting Agenda and Notes Format

Agenda Item	Time for Item	Decision Made	Person(s) Responsible	Date to Be Completed

Leadership Team Meeting Notes

Date: **Time:**   **In Attendance:**

Critical Outcomes for This Meeting:

AGENDA

Topic/Issue	Next Steps	Person Responsible	Timeline

Follow Up From Prior Meetings and Delegation:

Reflection on This Meeting:

- Consistent with our norms?
- Productive and efficient?
- Are we following through?

THE LEADER-FOLLOWER RELATIONSHIP

Our leadership team meetings just seem to go on and on. We never get closure and it feels like we are wasting time. I really resent this; I have so many more important things to do.

I don't think that Sherill knows how teachers feel about her. They think that she is aloof and doesn't care about them or their students. She is going to have a very hard time getting them to buy into this new idea.

Fred doesn't seem to assert himself with the district office. The DO could and should be so much more supportive but Fred won't demand the kind of support and responsiveness we need from the DO if we are going to do our job for kids.

—Voices of assistant principals

The danger in the leader-follower relationship is the assumption that the leader-follower relationship must dominate. If this assumption exists on the part of either the leader or the follower, they are both at risk. The leader's openness to diversity, empowering others, breakthrough thinking, and being challenged and learning from followers will drop precipitously. Followers will abandon their unique perspectives and healthy dissension, which are at the heart of the creative process and innovation.

—Ira Chaleff, *The Courageous Follower*

Background

If you are a principal, you should be acutely aware that your assistant principals potentially

- are closer to some teachers, students, and parents than you are, and are privy to knowledge and perceptions that you are otherwise unable to access.
- have knowledge of school and district culture, history, and politics that you don't.
- have a better sense of how you are being perceived by those around you than you do.
- are privy to the degree to which your ideas are being embraced and implemented.
- have intimate knowledge of your strengths and your weaknesses.
- have ears to the gossip network.
- are approached for end-runs that reveal much about school culture and systems.
- are the first to know if the emperor (that would be you) has no clothes.
- may be busy covering for your errors and omissions.
- are attuned to opportunities, needs, and priorities that you are blind to.
- are your best source of data and analysis about your school and about your own performance.

If you are an assistant principal, you know all of the above. You should also know

- the best measure of your success is the success of your school and its leadership team. You cannot isolate yourself from your principal's weaknesses.
- you have a moral and professional responsibility to come forward with your perceptions, concerns, and ideas.
- the best way you can support your school and your principal is through courageous followership.

In his book *The Courageous Follower*, Ira Chaleff (1995) suggests that there are five dimensions to courageous followership:

1. The courage to assume responsibility

2. The courage to serve

3. The courage to challenge

4. The courage to participate in transformation

5. The courage to take moral action

He ends his book with an admonishment to leaders to have the courage to listen to followers.

We are all both leaders and followers, often within the same institution. A principal may be the leader of the department chairs group, but may serve as a follower on a committee charged with making a textbook adoption. The principal may be a leader for a district task force, and a follower on a negotiations team. An assistant principal may be a leader among other assistant principals in organizing graduation, but a follower in developing a master schedule. Both roles are critical in schools. And while schools may be organized in a hierarchical fashion, they are not "command and control" organizations like the military or law enforcement. Healthy schools are grounded in collaborative, democratic cultures that are conducive to courageous followership.

Healthy principal/assistant principal relationships are grounded in common purpose. That purpose is not "to make the principal look good." It's not to "stay below the district office's radar and off the front page of the paper." Hopefully, the common purpose shared by principal and assistant principal is student success, and is articulated as a shared vision as discussed elsewhere in this book. Principal, if you are going to lead your school in pursuit of that common purpose, you have to create a culture, climate, and relationships in which courageous followership is the norm.

Discussion Questions

- What are some of the leader and follower roles that each of you serves in?
- Share an example of when you spoke up or acted as a courageous follower.

- For each of you, what do Chaleff's five dimensions of followership look like? What do you expect from your followers when you are in a leadership role, and from your leaders when you are in a followership role?

Shared Activities

- The principal identifies an area for his or her own professional growth and asks that the assistant provide feedback and coaching. This might involve the assistant observing the principal acting in some leadership role, with the assistant collecting objective data on the principal's performance and providing the principal with frank feedback.
- Build in an agenda item titled "courageous followership" at your regular leadership team meetings, where each of you solicits explicit feedback from one another around your exercise of leadership.

Activities for the AP

- Make a list for yourself of the characteristics and behaviors you admire in your principal and that you would like to emulate. Next, list those characteristics and behaviors of your principal that get in the way of his or her success. If your relationship is an open and trusting one, discuss the lists with your principal. If it isn't, shred 'em. And look for safe opportunities to provide your principal with specific and constructive feedback.
- Share the concept of courageous followership with a group you lead or supervise, and ask the group for frank and ongoing feedback.

Additional Resources

Chaleff, I. (1995). *The courageous follower.* San Francisco: Berrett-Koehler.

BUILDING AN APPRENTICESHIP PLAN

Got to pay your dues if you're going to sing the blues and you know it don't come easy.

—Ringo Starr

Background

The story is all too familiar. An assistant principal spends two or three years doing little more than student discipline. She is smart, skilled, and well regarded. She receives very little in the way of targeted feedback. She is drafted into a principalship, never having managed a budget or led an instructional initiative. Assuming her new principalship, she is staggered, never having imagined some of the issues that come across her desk. She's busy—too busy for the sort of stuff she did as an AP. If she never again has to investigate the source of cigarette smoke in a bathroom, it will be OK with her. She has her assistant principal handle all of the discipline, so she can do the "leadership stuff."

It's time for us to break that pattern. You can make your school a more successful institution by strengthening your leadership team, nurturing reflective practice and ongoing professional development on the part of the principal, and preparing the assistant principal for a principalship through a deliberate apprenticeship program. It's a win-win.

The tools in this book will support you in implementing an apprenticeship plan. In essence, what we offer here are lesson plans: topics, discussion questions, activities, and tools that you may use to strengthen your apprenticeship program. However, lesson plans are not enough; just as a teacher brings lessons to an annual plan built around goals, assessments, and individual relationships with her students, there are some basic commitments and mechanisms that must be in place if your principal/assistant principal relationship is to reach its full potential.

Before you take on the topical material in Parts II and III, we believe it is essential that you do the following:

Assess needs: Your plan should be grounded in an assessment of school needs and priorities, the principal's needs for support, and the learning and growth needs of the assistant principal. The needs identified in each of these areas need not come out of thin air. School needs and priorities should be clearly articulated in a school plan. In a healthy school, the plan provides clear direction for leadership. The principal's need for support should be derived from the school plan, as well as from the principal's summative evaluation and personal goals and objectives. The assistant principal's learning and growth needs should be identified through self-evaluation, and in collaboration with the principal. We have provided you with several tools that may assist you in a needs assessment process.

Establish explicit goals: The assistant principal should have clear professional development and work goals tied to the needs assessment discussed above. Where there is a solid evaluation system in place that requires the establishment of goals, no duplication of effort should be required; these are the goals for the apprenticeship plan. For those of you in systems without established processes or formats, we have provided a simple tool for goal setting.

Outline a one- or two-year schedule: As we have discussed, in the traditional haphazard model, assistant principals spend their time doing discipline and "pick-up." We are suggesting that APs rotate through a series of responsibilities so they can develop the full spectrum of school leadership knowledge and skills. This rotation should be planned out over the course of one or two years, and must be done in coordination with others on the leadership team, including the principal, other assistants, resource teachers, and the like. Again, we have provided a simple tool that you may find useful in identifying key areas of responsibility and building a timeline, linked to the topical areas outlined in this book.

Establish regular meeting times: Everything about the life of a school administrator conspires against your efforts to meet and to focus those meetings on these issues. However, meeting regularly to build and manage your apprenticeship relationship is the single most important thing you can do if you intend to pursue the goals we have discussed above. Build a schedule, stick to it, and don't allow tactical issues to consume your time and attention.

Regularly evaluate your progress: Think of your relationship as a continuous improvement process, one in which you are constantly monitoring and adjusting your collaborative work. Every meeting should include a brief, informal check-in, and on something like a quarterly basis, you should schedule a more in-depth review. *The Meeting Agenda/Record* form may help you to structure and sustain these conversations.

Commit to the relationship: In traditional apprenticeship models, there is a contract between master and apprentice. The apprentice agrees to sacrifice time, labor, earnings, and sometimes freedom for several years of service to the master. The master, in exchange, agrees to prepare the apprentice for membership in the guild, craft, or profession.

Contrast this relationship with the typical supervisor/supervisee relationship. In this relationship the employee is expected to perform specified tasks for agreed upon compensation. Period. The employer provides the context in which the employee can do his or her work, and provides direction and compensation, with little attention to the employee's growth and development beyond his or her current position.

As we have stated, we are suggesting that you enter into a relationship that is deliberately designed to improve the effectiveness of both parties, and to prepare the apprentice to at least figuratively take over the job of the master. This is a significant commitment, and a deviation from the norm. We believe it merits the endorsement of a formal written agreement by both parties. A sample agreement is included.

Discussion Questions

- What are each of your personal goals and timelines in relation to your careers? How can you support one another in achieving those goals in a variety of scenarios?

Shared Activities

- Discuss, revise as appropriate, and sign the *Principal/Assistant Principal Apprenticeship Agreement* as a document that will guide your relationship.
- Individually complete the *Self-Assessment in Relation to ISLLC Standards* that follows in the Tools section. Share and discuss your reflections, and use this discussion to inform your goal setting process.
- Develop goals using the *Goal Setting Worksheet* provided or the goal forms in your district's evaluation process. Ensure that your goals are complementary.
- Use the *Aligning School, Principal, and Assistant Principal Needs to Build an Apprenticeship Plan* form to identify areas of responsibility for the AP that will support the principal and school, and contribute to the AP's growth.
- Complete an *Annual Rotation Plan* in collaboration with the entire leadership team to ensure that individual administrators experience a wide spectrum of responsibilities of the course of a one- or two-year period.

Activities for the AP

- Ensure that your progress in this process is a topic that is revisited with your principal on a regular basis.

Additional Resources

ISLLC. (2008). *Standards*. Washington, DC: Council of Chief State School Officers. Retrieved August 10, 2008, from http://www.ccsso.org/projects/Interstate_Consortium_on_School_Leadership/ISLLC_Standards/

Marzano, R. I., Water, T., & McNulty, B. (2005). *School leadership that works: From research to results*. Alexandria, VA: Association for Supervision and Curriculum Development.

Tools

- Principal/Assistant Principal Apprenticeship Agreement
- Self-Assessment in Relation to the ISLLC Standards
- Goal Setting Worksheet
- Aligning School, Principal, and Assistant Principal Needs to Build an Apprenticeship Plan
- Annual Rotation Plan
- Meeting Agenda/Record

Principal/Assistant Principal Apprenticeship Agreement

We commit to the following shared goals and processes:

- To work together as a team to provide effective leadership for our school
- To deliberately manage our relationship so that we both grow professionally as a result
- To maintain open, honest, and consistent communication with one another
- To meet on a scheduled, weekly basis for mentoring conversations based upon the content of this book, other professional growth activities, and to problem solve around school-related issues and responsibilities
- To meet on a quarterly basis to review the AP's goals, responsibilities, and professional growth in a conscious effort to expand the AP's range of knowledge and experience
- To consciously manage our relationship and the AP's responsibilities to develop the AP's capacity to assume a principalship in the coming years

Responsibilities of the Principal

- To assign responsibilities that allow the AP to focus on a limited number of tasks and to vary the tasks over time in order to expose the AP to a wide spectrum of responsibilities
- To commit to mentoring the assistant principal as a future site principal

Responsibilities of the Assistant Principal

- To seek professional development opportunities that broaden exposure to a full range of dispositions, knowledge, and abilities required of school leaders
- To set personal goals that will lead to growth as a future principal
- To be a "courageous follower," committed to the success of the principal and the effectiveness of the site

Principal Signature _____

Assistant Principal Signature _____

Weekly meeting day and time:

Quarterly meeting dates and times:

Self-Assessment in Relation to the ISLLC Standards

An education leader promotes the success of every student by	What successes have you experienced this year?	What challenges do you still face?	What professional development needs do you have?
1. Facilitating the development, articulation, implementation, and stewardship of a vision of learning that is shared and supported by the school community.			
2. Advocating, nurturing, and sustaining a school culture and instructional program conducive to student learning and staff professional growth.			
3. Ensuring management of the organization, operations, and resources for a safe, efficient, and effective learning environment.			
4. Collaborating with families and community members, responding to diverse community needs, and mobilizing community resources.			
5. Modeling a personal code of ethics and developing professional leadership capacity.			
6. Understanding, responding to, and influencing the larger political, social, economic, legal, and cultural context.			

29

Goal Setting Worksheet

PROGRAM GOAL

Key Objectives	Critical Activities	Timeline

PROGRAM GOAL

Key Objectives	Critical Activities	Timeline

PROGRAM GOAL

Key Objectives	Critical Activities	Timeline

Strengths	Areas for Growth

PROFESSIONAL GROWTH GOAL(S)

Action Plan	What Might Be Evidence of Growth?

Aligning School, Principal, and Assistant Principal Needs to Build an Apprenticeship Plan

School Need/ Priority	Support Needed by Principal to Address Need/ Priority	Learning Needs and Leadership Opportunities for AP in Need/ Priority Area	Apprenticeship Activities

Annual Rotation Plan			
ISLLC Standard Area	**Topic/Focus**	**AP Responsibilities**	**Timeline**
1. Facilitating the development, articulation, implementation, and stewardship of a vision of learning that is shared and supported by the school community.			
2. Advocating, nurturing, and sustaining a school culture and instructional program conducive to student learning and staff professional growth.			
3. Ensuring management of the organization, operations, and resources for a safe, efficient, and effective learning environment.			
4. Collaborating with families and community members, responding to diverse community needs, and mobilizing community resources.			
5. Modeling a personal code of ethics and developing professional leadership capacity.			
6. Understanding, responding to, and influencing the larger political, social, economic, legal, and cultural context.			

Meeting Agenda/Record

Date:

Area of Responsibility	Progress	Challenges	Learning	Next Steps

Action steps for principal:

Next steps, upcoming new responsibilities in apprenticeship plan:

Key topics for review at next meeting:

Next meeting date:

What is working in this relationship; how can it be improved?

THE MANAGERIAL BASICS OF SCHOOL LEADERSHIP

The relevant question for the learning organization is not, "Who is in charge?" but rather, "How can we best get results?"
—DuFour & Eaker, *Professional Learning Communities at Work*, 1998

Teachers teach best when they are known well, when expectations are high and support is focused and purposeful, and when their voices are valued. Skillful leaders spend lots of time with teachers, focusing conversations and classroom observations on teaching and learning. Skillful leaders develop systems that make the organization run smoothly so that teachers have the time and resources to teach well. Teachers will not cooperate with administrators unless the school climate feels safe and orderly, and clearly values teaching and learning.

In this part of the book, we focus on the management functions of school leaders—that is, how leaders develop systems that deal effectively with the recurring functions of the job.

No school leader or leadership team will succeed if it hasn't mastered the basic management processes and skills that underlie any effective school. These areas are typically among the very first to challenge a new assistant principal. They represent skills that are hard to teach in preservice programs, and are thus prime ground for your apprenticeship relationship.

TIME MANAGEMENT

Time is an illusion. Lunchtime doubly so.

—Douglas Adams

Background

Time is the single greatest source of frustration for principals and assistant principals. There simply isn't enough of it. The average full-time worker in the United States works just under forty hours a week, while workers in France, Denmark, and other European countries work around thirty-five. You? If you are an average school administrator, you are working somewhere around fifty-five hours a week. Despite the excessive—yes, excessive—hours you work, odds are you complain that you don't have enough time for your most important priorities: visiting classrooms, coaching teachers, and leading school improvement. We won't even mention unattended and trivial needs such as eating and sleeping, family, exercise, and having your oil changed and teeth cleaned.

We are not hourly workers. We are public servants, and the best of us are fueled by moral purpose and love for our profession. We are not clock-watchers; we are professionals. Nonetheless, it is critically important that your principal/assistant principal team attend to time in a very deliberate way for two reasons:

1. Odds are, you are spending time doing things that will not make significant contributions to the realization of your vision for your school, and are neglecting things that would.

2. Odds are, you are neglecting personal relationships, exercise, and other important facets of your life. This neglect threatens your effectiveness and longevity as a school leader.

It is the nature of school leadership that the job is never finished. When we were classroom teachers, we could firm up tomorrow's lesson plans, correct papers, turn off the lights, and go home. As principals, however, there is almost always something else that could be done, another meeting to attend, another memo to read, another game to make an appearance at, or another pile to organize. Competing priorities and the impossibility of daily closure conspire to stress us and rob our personal time. Effective time managers learn to set boundaries around personal and professional time. They learn to establish and maintain firm priorities around how they spend time in personal and professional domains. They don't allow themselves to become victims; they manage time as a resource.

There is more variation among adults in the speed with which they complete tasks than in their ability to complete those tasks. One of the best ways you can make time for instructional leadership is by becoming more efficient, faster. And because principals spend the majority of their time interacting with other people, this means that you have to become more

efficient in your meetings and conversations. For many school leaders this is a difficult assignment. We think of ourselves as "people persons" and we want folks to feel welcome and listened to when they come to us with a need or problem. But if you step back from many of the conversations that take place in the principal's office, you will see that they often meander and loop, covering the same ground multiple times and accomplishing little. It is reasonable and legitimate for you as a professional to tell a parent that you have fifteen minutes to hear out his or her concern. It is important for you to recognize that the ten minutes you shave off of six conversations during the course of a day provides you with thirty more minutes to spend in classrooms and thirty more minutes to spend with your family.

It is virtually impossible to succeed as a school leader without implementing an effective system of to-do lists, schedules, and calendars. Assistant principals are often not prepared for the complex multitude of demands that come with the position; principals can be of tremendous assistance by modeling the ways they manage to keep all of those plates in the air.

There is no one right system for calendar and to-do list management; paper calendars, PDAs, and Web-based systems all have advantages and disadvantages. Whatever system you use, we believe that it is critical that you

- block out sacrosanct time for "important, not urgent" tasks such as classroom walkthroughs, school plan development, and professional reading;
- maintain daily and long-term to-do lists that are reviewed and updated every day;
- set up to-do lists so that recurring tasks (e.g., monthly or annually) are posted automatically and recurring work products (e.g., your annual announcement for open house) are filed and readily accessible; and
- backward-plan the tasks required for the completion of projects, post those subtasks on to-do lists, and block time for their completion on your calendar.

Steven Covey (1996) has developed a conceptual framework that we believe is a powerful tool in our time management struggle. Covey suggests the way we spend our time can be divided into four categories: activities that are important and urgent, important and not urgent, not important and not urgent, and not important and urgent. We suggest that for the purpose of your explorations of time management, we define as important *those tasks and responsibilities that are likely to make a sustained and significant contribution to student achievement and that depend on positional leadership for their accomplishment.* By that definition, dealing with one irate parent may be urgent, but it is not likely to be important. In what quadrant would you place meeting with a salesman, conducting classroom walkthroughs, discussing student work in a department meeting, supervising in the cafeteria . . . ? You may feel like you accomplished a lot checking the day's quadrants 1, 3, and 4 tasks off of your to-do list, but in the end you may have accomplished very little in the way of leadership activities that will have an impact on student achievement.

The power of the four-quadrants model lies in the recognition that we neglect the "important, not urgent" tasks and responsibilities, and that it is action in this very quadrant that keeps things from rising to the level of urgency. It is action in this proactive and strategic quadrant that drives genuine school improvement.

Covey's Quadrants

Important Urgent 1	Important Not Urgent 2
Not Important Urgent 3	Not Important Not Urgent 4

Discussion Questions

- What systems are you using to manage your to-do lists, schedules, and calendars? What are the strengths and challenges of these systems, and how might you improve them?
- What parameters should each of you set in relation to the hours that you work? How can you manage daily hours, night, and weekend responsibilities in a fair and sustainable way?
- How does the way you spend your time reflect your priorities? How can you use other resources and people to protect your time and support your priorities?
- How can you support one another in meeting your time management goals?

Shared Activities

- Use the *Daily Log* to record, on a ten-minute by ten-minute basis, how you spend your time in the course of two randomly selected days in a two-week period. For the balance of days during that period, including weekend days, reconstruct your time utilization at the end of each day. Highlight time spent on "important, not urgent" tasks. Interview each other about your time logs. Do the time logs provide evidence that you are focusing your energies on vision and priorities for the school? Do your logs align with the twenty-one McREL leadership responsibilities and/or with the ISLLC standards? Resolve, in writing, to make some changes in how you use your time, and repeat the logging process in three months to evaluate your success in implementing any changes.

- Identify an "urgent, important" category of tasks that is taking a significant portion of your time. Use the *Task Analysis Worksheet* to do the "important, not urgent" work of developing a system or solution that will take some of these issues off of your plates.
- Observe one another dealing with discipline incidents and conferencing with parents and teachers. Debrief the observation around the effectiveness of the interaction, and also around its efficiency. Would additional preparation have made for a more efficient conversation? Could similar outcomes have been reached in less time?

Activities for the AP

- Experiment with the following: When a parent, student, or teacher asks to speak with you regarding a problem or a need,
  o rather than deal with the issue immediately, make an appointment at a time that will not interrupt your other duties.
  o set a time parameter for the conversation, e.g., "I have ten minutes. Can we resolve this in that amount of time?"
  o establish the desired outcome at the start of the conversation, e.g., "What do you hope we can produce in this conversation?"
  o summarize any next steps at the end of the conversation, e.g., "OK, so you're going to call Mrs. Jones, and I'll have the registrar correct the transcript."

- Use the *Task Analysis Worksheet* to determine the subtasks required to complete a project. Enter those subtasks onto your calendar and to-do lists.

Additional Resources

Covey, Stephen R. (1996). *First things first*. New York: Fireside.

Tools

- Daily Log
- Task Analysis Worksheet

Daily Log

Record in intervals as fine-grained as ten minutes.

Date: Page:

Time	Task	Covey Quad*	Relationship to Instructional Leadership and Strategic Plan	Comments

*Important, Urgent = 1; Important, Not Urgent = 2; Not Important, Urgent = 3; Not Important, Not Urgent = 4

Task Analysis Worksheet

Step 1: Through the *Daily Log* exercise or in discussion, identify a task or category of activities that is consuming a disproportionate amount of your time that is not in the "important, not urgent" category, and that is not closely tied to instructional leadership and your school's strategic plan. We'll call this a *Time Eating Task*.

Step 2: Estimate the number of hours or minutes each week your leadership team spends on this *Time Eating Task*.

Step 3: List at least three other tasks or responsibilities your team could be spending this time on—tasks that would more directly contribute to academic achievement, your vision for your school, and that fall into the "important, not urgent" category.

1.
2.
3.

Step 4: Your *Time Eating Task* is generated as the result of a problem or need. Use the "*seven whys method*" to unpack the sources of the task. Get to the root of the problem or need by questioning the *why* through at least seven layers as you dig though the issue.

1.   4.   6.
2.   5.   7.
3.

Step 5: As you examine the underlying issues that are driving your *Time Eating Task,* identify a few places where you might set up systems that would prevent the issue from developing or getting to your desk. Don't forget to delegate where appropriate.

Step 6: Commit to establishing the rules, systems, or procedures that will keep the *Time Eating Task* from monopolizing your time. In following up on this, note who is doing what by when, and how you are going to follow up to ensure implementation and to evaluate that implementation.

Step 7: Go back to Step 3; how are you going to reallocate your time to more strategic activities?

Task Analysis Worksheet
SAMPLE

Step 1: Through the *Daily Log* exercise or in discussion, identify a task or category of activities that is consuming a disproportionate amount of your time that is not in the "important, not urgent" category, and that is not closely tied to instructional leadership and your school's strategic plan. We'll call this a *Time Eating Task*.

Our three assistant principals are spending a large amount of time supervising at lunch and breaks.

Step 2: Estimate the number of hours or minutes each week your leadership team spends on this *Time Eating Task*.

The three APs are spending a combined total of about thirty hours a week on lunch and break supervision.

Step 3: List at least three other tasks or responsibilities your team could be spending this time on—tasks that would more directly contribute to academic achievement, your vision for your school, and that fall into the "important, not urgent" category.

We are not getting into classrooms enough, and need more time to conference with teachers and department chairs. We still haven't completed our analysis of the spring test data.

Step 4: Your *Time Eating Task* is generated as the result of a problem or need. Use the "*seven whys method*" to unpack the sources of the task. Get to the root of the problem or need by questioning the *why* through at least seven layers as you dig though the issue.

We're all out on supervision because we think we are important to safety, we are important to safety because adult supervision is critical, we are the adults because teachers get a break, aides and campus supervisors don't do it alone because they can't handle it, they can't handle it because they haven't been trained, they haven't been trained because we don't have clear supervision procedures . . .

Step 5: As you examine the underlying issues that are driving your *Time Eating Task*, identify a few places where you might set up systems that would prevent the issue from developing or getting to your desk. Don't forget to delegate where appropriate.

Perhaps if we develop clearer procedures around supervision zones, use of the radios, and spend some time training the campus supervisors and aides, only one of the three of us will need to be in the yard on any one break.

Step 6: Commit to establishing the rules, systems, or procedures that will keep the *Time Eating Task* from monopolizing your time. In following up on this, note who is doing what by when, and how you are going to follow up to ensure implementation and to evaluate that implementation.

Joe and Sue will bring a plan back to us by our next weekly meeting that will allow us to pilot a one AP on the yard model. The plan will address supervision zones, scheduling, and training for classified staff.

Step 7: Go back to Step 3; how are you going to reallocate your time to more strategic activities?

Our goal in implementing this plan will be for each AP to do at least five more short classroom observations and two more teacher conferences a week. We will evaluate implementation of this plan in two months.

DELEGATION

1. Always say "we."

2. Create interactions.

3. Create a climate of trust. Delegation is fundamentally a system of trust. You signal your trust in someone when you truly delegate authority to that person. Every leader ought to have an established system of delegation. If not, we suggest you establish one right now.

4. Focus on gains, not losses.

5. Involve people in planning and problem solving.
   - Select people with a working knowledge of the situation.
   - Clearly articulate outcomes to be met.
   - Provide resources and authority to do the job.
   - Set up a timetable for planning and problem solving.
   - Enable information flow upward as well as downward.
   - Periodically review progress with the groups.
     —Kouzes & Pozner, *The Leadership Challenge*, 1992

Background

Schools are complex organizations in which hundreds of people work together toward common ends. A school leader might be thought of as an orchestra conductor: an individual charged with bringing a diverse group of musicians together to produce a performance that is true to a vision derived from the work of the composer, the conductor, and the musicians themselves. The conductor can't produce the work alone, and may not be able to play any one instrument as well as any individual member of the orchestra. Yet the conductor ensures that all the players are in place, know their parts, and know when and how to play them as part of a larger community of artists.

Organizations often stumble due to the lack of an effective conductor. Individuals are not sure what music they are playing, what section of the orchestra they are seated in, what their part is, how and when to play it, and how to judge the quality of their contribution. As principal and assistant principal, you are conductor and first violin in your building. Here we explore the topic of delegation, in the hope that things at your school will become a bit more on tempo and in tune.

In the course of a typical hour on the job, chances are you have done some or all of the following:
- Asked that a student be brought to the office so you can follow through on a discipline question
- Asked a secretary to send out a memo
- Left a note for a teacher requesting that he meet with you
- Called the district office about a personnel question
- Asked the activities director to coordinate an upcoming dance
- Received an e-mail from the district office about an upcoming meeting

Each of these interactions has the potential to produce sour notes.

- The student is pulled from class in the middle of an important test.
- The memo was e-mailed without being proofread.
- The teacher misinterpreted your request as an attack on his competence.
- The district office got back to you too late to meet your needs.
- The activities director mistakenly assumed that you will arrange for security at the dance.
- The district office was upset because your assistant principals didn't attend the curriculum meeting.

Your work life centers on the coordination of shared work, and the responsibilities that members of your organization share with one another. Breakdowns often occur when that coordination is haphazard and when responsibilities are unclear.

The concept of workflow is one way of thinking about the delegation and coordination of responsibilities within an organization. It is a deceptively simple way of thinking about how we can work together more harmoniously. Like many "habits of mind," workflow is easy to understand, but takes discipline to make operational.

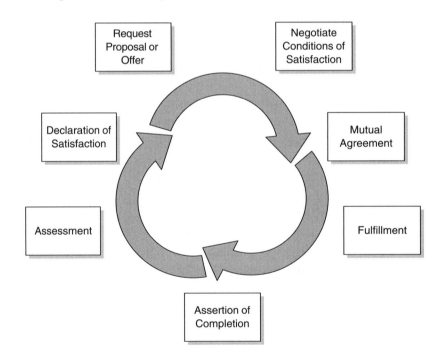

The workflow model suggests that the successful accomplishment of any task that involves two or more entities can be broken down into seven stages:

1. *The expression of a request, proposal, or offer.* Two parties may begin to work together after any of these three actions, but delegation is usually initiated through a request. This first stage of the process is often where delegation breaks down. It is not unusual for someone to think that she has made a request, but the listener does not interpret

the statement in the same way. Sue says to her custodian, "The girl's room is dirty," thinking the custodian understands that she is asking him to clean the restroom. The custodian, on the other hand, doesn't hear a request, he hears the principal commiserating about slovenly students.

2. *Negotiation of conditions of satisfaction.* The two parties clarify what is meant by the request: What will be done, by whom, to what standards, and when? What kinds of support are needed and offered? This is the stage of the process that is often omitted, and is the source of most of the problems we experience in delegation. For example, Sue may make an explicit request of the custodian that he clean the restroom, leaving plenty of room for uncertainty, poor performance, or even conflict. Sue's version of "clean" may include checking and filling the soap dispensers; the custodian's may not. Sue may assume that the job will occur before the next recess, the custodian may assume that he can get to the job later, after he does the assembly set-up that Sue had requested earlier. At this stage of the process, then, it is critical that both parties have a clear understanding of what is being requested, proposed, or offered. There can be give and take around defining the task and its timeline, and the roles that both parties and others might play in completing the task.

3. *Mutual agreement.* The parties acknowledge that the conditions of satisfaction are understood, and explicitly agree to meet them. An informal contract has been negotiated; a promise has been made.

4. *Fulfillment.* The parties act on their commitments. Even in a delegation scenario, the delegator may have responsibilities along with the delegatee. For instance, in the case of Sue and her custodian, Sue has agreed to arrange for the custodian to receive help in setting up for the assembly.

5. *Assertion of completion.* Steps 5, 6, and 7 are frequently omitted from our delegation processes, but these are the steps where learning takes place, and where organizational growth occurs. These steps make the workflow model one of continuous improvement. In Step 5, the delegatee lets the delegator know that he has completed the task, "OK, I have completed the work I agreed to do for you."

6. *Assessment.* The parties review the previously-agreed-upon conditions of satisfaction, and determine if they have been met. They examine the work product against their standards, and if they have been met, the stage is set for . . .

7. *Declaration of satisfaction.* The parties close the loop on the workflow. The delegator declares that the task is complete to his or her satisfaction, or, if not, the parties have an opportunity to capture learning that will drive improvement the next time the task needs to be completed. The delegatee receives acknowledgment and feedback that will contribute to future performance.

Effective delegation and shared leadership are critically important to your success as a school leadership team. Delegation builds the capacity of those around you, creates buy in, and allows you to be more productive and to focus your energy on your top priority, which has to be instruction. We can't tell you how many times we have met with principals and assistant principals who tell us they don't have the time to get into classrooms to coach teachers and supervise instruction, yet they are spending hours as bookkeepers, yard supervisors, maintenance heads, and "go-fers."

Discussion Questions

- Discuss a few situations where delegation and workflow have worked well at your school, and a few situations in which they have broken down.
- How is workflow working within your own team? Think of both positive and less than positive examples and analyze them against the seven workflow steps.

Shared Activities

- Use the *Workflow Worksheet* to manage a delegated responsibility within your own leadership team.
- Refer back to the previous chapter on time management. Review Covey's Four Quadrants, and identify at least three "urgent, important" or "urgent, not important" tasks that have kept you away from classrooms and other "not urgent, important" work the past few weeks. Develop systems that will allow you to delegate these tasks, and outline a process to do so using workflow.

Activities for the AP

- Train other individuals at your site who are responsible for supervision and/or delegation in workflow (lead custodian, department chairs, head librarian, office manager, etc.) and ask them to implement the concept with their colleagues.

Tools

- Workflow Worksheet

Workflow Worksheet

Step 1: What is the task at hand?

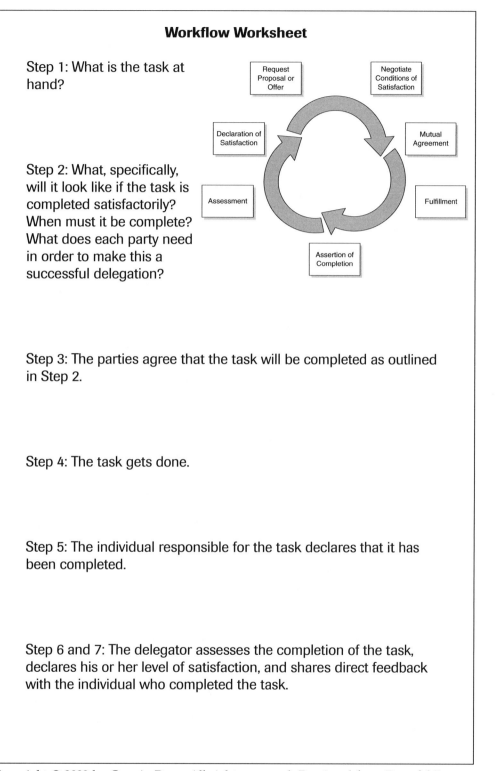

Step 2: What, specifically, will it look like if the task is completed satisfactorily? When must it be complete? What does each party need in order to make this a successful delegation?

Step 3: The parties agree that the task will be completed as outlined in Step 2.

Step 4: The task gets done.

Step 5: The individual responsible for the task declares that it has been completed.

Step 6 and 7: The delegator assesses the completion of the task, declares his or her level of satisfaction, and shares direct feedback with the individual who completed the task.

STUDENT DISCIPLINE

*The great end of education is to discipline rather than to furnish the mind; to train
it to the use of its own powers, rather than fill it with the accumulation of others.*

—Tryon Edwards

Background

Despite all of the rhetoric about instructional leadership, and the
ninety-three "performances" that the ISLLC standards hold school leaders
responsible for, most principals and assistant principals spend the plural-
ity, if not the majority, of their time dealing with student discipline and student activities. It goes without saying that students learn best when they
are undistracted and feel safe, both in classrooms and on the campus.
Teachers teach best when they are assured that students behave appropriately in the classroom and on campus and that they will be supported
when students violate behavioral expectations. Teachers would tell us that
dealing effectively with student discipline is a prerequisite to instructional
leadership. Research confirms that notion. The McREL meta-analysis of
leadership behaviors correlated with high student achievement found that
effective principals "protect teachers from issues and influences that
would detract from their teaching time and focus" (p. 48).

Despite the importance of student discipline and the huge bite it takes
out of school administrators' time, it is a topic that is barely touched upon
in administration preservice programs. One of our colleagues is half serious when she says that she would have been better prepared for her real
work as an assistant principal had she attended the FBI academy than she
was attending a local university's school administration program.

Almost every assistant principal has major responsibilities in the area
of student discipline. Principals typically rely on APs to manage day-to-
day discipline. They expect parents and students to experience a system
that is consistent and fair. They should not, however, assume they can simply hand their APs a stack of suspension forms and get out of the way.
Principals should take an active role in establishing the school culture and
expectations around discipline and in mentoring their APs in carrying out
discipline processes. Principals should not expect their APs to do "all discipline, all of the time"; principals should do their share as well, so that APs
have the time and opportunity to take on other responsibilities, and so that
they maintain hands-on experience with the process. Assistant principals
easily become inundated in their role as "campus cop" and find little time
to establish systems that help alleviate student misbehavior. As a result
they find little time to learn to be a school leader. Principals who do not
participate in discipline become distant from daily school interactions and
culture, and isolated in their offices and off-campus activities.

Following are a few considerations we think should inform your
team's conversations about student discipline.

- The amount of time that you spend on discipline, and the nature of the problems you deal with, is largely determined by your school's culture and expectations. Investments of time in culture building will pay huge dividends in the prevention of discipline problems and tasks.
- Clear, logical, explicit, and highly consistent rules and procedures are critical to effective student discipline. Designing, evaluating, and adjusting these systems is an often neglected but essential "important, not urgent" task.
- Effective teachers who build relationships with students and who take responsibility for discipline are at the heart of school cultures that minimize discipline issues. On an hour-by-hour basis, you will do more to improve discipline at your site by supervising and supporting quality teaching than you will by supervising students.
- Many school discipline processes are self-defeating: suspensions that result in amplified cycles of student failure, tardy policies that lock kids out of class, and practices that are designed for the convenience of adults rather than in the interest of students.
- You are in this business to be an educator, not a law enforcement officer.

Discussion Questions

- What's currently working, and what's not, for student discipline at your school?
- What are the principal's expectations around how APs handle student discipline? How consistent are you being in the implementation of your discipline expectations and plan?
- How can you take steps to minimize discipline incidents and the time you spend on discipline?

Shared Activities

- Complete the *Student Discipline Assessment Worksheet* and develop an action plan as a result of your findings.
- Review data related to student discipline such as suspensions, detentions, tardies, and attendance at your monthly team meetings and track that data in relation to the impact of your initiatives.
- Observe one another conducting discipline-related activities such as interviewing students or conferencing with parents in order to give each other feedback on efficiency and to ensure consistent practice.

Activities for the AP

- Review teacher referral data and identify the three teachers that generate the most referrals. Conduct frequent observations in these

teachers' classrooms and coach (or direct) them to improve their
management skills and take responsibility for student discipline.

• Identify a particular source of disciplinary problems outside of the
classroom; it might be a particular group of students, certain activity, or zone on your campus. Consult with others and implement
and evaluate a plan to improve disciplinary outcomes.

Tools

• Student Discipline Assessment Worksheet

Student Discipline Assessment Worksheet

1. What does our data tell us about year-to-year trends and comparisons to similar schools in suspensions, expulsions, detentions, attendance, tardies, and graduation rates? What do we learn when we disaggregate these data by gender, grade, ethnicity, and other relevant variables?

2. How would an informed outsider characterize our school culture around discipline?

3. How have we intervened to build a positive culture around discipline?

4. Do we have a behavior code with specific consequences for specific behaviors? Are the behaviors and consequences explicit, known by all, realistic, and productive?

5. Do teachers share in discipline responsibilities such that first and minor infractions are dealt with by the teacher? Are teachers expected to contact parents for first and minor infractions? Is this happening with consistency?

6. How are we dealing with faculty, administration, and staff who are not consistently carrying out their responsibilities in relation to the behavior code?

7. Which teachers make the most referrals and why? What support is given to these teachers so that fewer referrals will be made?

8. Which students are given the most referrals? What does this say about whom the school serves well? What interventions are in place for these students, both socially and academically?

9. Is adequate and competent supervision provided on campus at appropriate times?

10. Are campus supervisors properly trained and supervised? What training is given to those who need additional skills?

11. Are teachers properly trained in classroom management skills? What professional development is given to those who need additional skills?

12. What system is in place to monitor student behavior and to communicate efficiently and effectively with parents, students, and teachers?

13. What are two specific steps we can take to improve our school culture and reduce disciplinary infractions?

14. What are two specific steps we can take to make our disciplinary process more likely to produce positive outcomes for our rule-breaking students?

15. What are two specific steps we can take to make our supervision and discipline processes more efficient and less likely to monopolize the time of our administrators?

16. How will we measure the impacts of the action plans we will develop around our answers to items 13, 14, and 15?

STUDENT ACTIVITIES

*We should use kids' positive states to draw them into learning in the domains
where they can develop competencies. . . . You learn at your best when you have
something you care about and can get pleasure from being engaged in.*

—Howard Gardner

Background

When most adults who liked school are asked for their fondest memories, their responses are almost always related to student activities rather than learning in classrooms. People talk about athletics, band, drama, dances, homecoming, etc. When adults who disliked school are asked for their least favorite memories, they are almost always associated with the alienation they felt related to these same activities. When student activities are led well, they are inclusive and purposefully designed as learning experiences for students. When student activities are led poorly, they involve a limited number of students and are primarily focused on winning in the case of athletics and on socializing in most other cases. As with student discipline, the role the assistant principal plays in leading and supporting student activities involves a lot of recurring tasks that are best dealt with when effective systems are put in place. Student activities always involve leadership roles for numerous adults and students, and when led well, many people feel empowered.

Cheerleading offers a classic illustration. Most high school and middle school principals talk with pain about the time spent monitoring cheerleader selection, relationships amongst cheerleaders, and the concerns of parents about the support desired for cheerleading. When skilled leadership is not in place, the complaints come to the principal and can overwhelm him or her with "urgent, unimportant" time eating tasks. When the selection process is determined collaboratively and followed consistently, when the cheerleading coach is skillful at communicating with students and teaches them conflict resolution skills, when parents are communicated with regularly, fewer problems arise and far less time is taken from other leadership tasks at the school.

In many cases the assistant principal is responsible for working with the cheerleading coach, and in other examples with the student leadership teacher, with the athletic coaches or at least with the athletic director, with the band teacher, etc. When the assistant principal is effective in working with these people, fewer problems arise and more time is available for other leadership work.

There are few cultural traditions as deeply embedded in our society as those surrounding high school activities and athletics. They are often the tail that wags the dog at secondary schools. In that light, following are a few considerations we think should inform your discussions around student activities.

- It is clear that students who participate in extracurricular activities are more likely to succeed in school. However, traditional activities often do not attract the participation of many students with different interests and/or backgrounds. Clubs and teams are often the most segregated sanctioned groups at a school. Schools need to be creative in recruiting student participation, in designing alternative activities, and in ensuring that *academic engagement* is at least as, if not more, esteemed in the school culture than athletic accomplishment.
- Athletics and activities often consume an inordinate amount of a school and its leadership team's time, resources, and energy. There are plenty of schools that claim their mission is academic, yet they focus their attention on a winning team, all the while producing appalling dropout rates and other academic measures. Your leadership team needs to be clear about its priorities and its vision for the role of athletics and activities, and to set reasonable limits and expectations around the investments you will make in this area relative to others.

Discussion Questions

- What is the purpose of student activities and athletics at your school relative to your mission and school plan? What evidence do you have that activities and athletics are supporting your mission and goals?
- What do you know about patterns of student participation? Which students are not participating, and what can you do to engage them in extracurricular activities?

Shared Activities

- Complete (with the assistance of staff) the *Activities Inventory Worksheet*, and work with staff and students to develop a plan to improve participation and cost effectiveness, and to design new activities that will build school culture and support the achievement of your mission.

Activities for the AP

- Design and sponsor a club or activity targeted at an underserved/underparticipating group of students.
- Conduct a series of focus groups with randomly selected students to assess their experience of your school's culture and activities. Report your findings to the student council and leadership team.

Tools

- Activities Inventory Worksheet

Activities Inventory Worksheet

Activity or Sports Name	Participant Data		Other Student Characteristics	Relation to School Mission	Evidence of Positive Impact on Students
	#	M/F	Ethnicity			

SITE BUDGET MANAGEMENT

Money alone sets all the world in motion.

—Publilius Syrus (~100 BC)

Background

Site principals have a high degree of budget authority, even in centralized school districts. They often don't use that authority, allowing the budget to operate on automatic pilot, maintaining the status quo, and failing to use the resources that the budget represents to support a school improvement agenda. It is not unusual for principals to keep the site budget in a "black box" or, at the very least, to hesitate to share budget knowledge and responsibilities with their assistant principals. This is not a surprise in a culture in which money is closely linked to power, but it is a mistake. Budget processes should be transparent and site leaders should not spend their time on the logistics of daily financial management.

A budget is much more than a spreadsheet; it is a planning and policy document that reflects a school's direction and priorities. It is a document that should be subject to regular review and revision, and that should be tightly linked to the school plan. Assistant principals, as instructional leaders at their sites and as future principals, should be actively engaged with the school budget.

Effective budget management rests on timely and accurate information about revenues and expenditures. Effective school leaders ensure that they have access to the budget information they need. They do not, however, fall into the trap of doing accounting work themselves; they make sure that budget systems are in place so they can make informed decisions while dedicating their time to instructional concerns.

Assistant principals should be fully included in budget development and management processes. They should understand district financial reporting and accountability systems. They should have decision-making authority in some project areas, so that when and if they move into principalship, they "know the ropes" around budgets.

Discussion Questions

- What is your site's annual budget? How do costs for certificated personnel, classified personnel, benefits, and nonpersonnel items break out?
- What is your budgetary decision-making process, and how is your budget linked to your school plan?
- What are your processes and guidelines around cash accounts, such as petty cash and student body funds?
- To what extent can you assert that funding at your school
  - is targeted at teaching and learning?
  - is distributed according to differential needs?
  - is reallocated based on evidence of impact?

Shared Activities

- Identify a particular program you would like to examine.
  - o Review the line-item budget.
  - o Review expenditures to date.
  - o What planning document and process drives this budget?
  - o What data constitutes evidence that this is money well spent? Can we make a direct link between this budget and student achievement?
  - o What is the decision-making process in relation to this budget?

- Develop a flow chart that describes your budget development process. Note the involved parties at each stage of the process, and links to district and school plans. Also chart budget tracking and purchasing processes. Identify those stages of the processes that require your leadership and stakeholder input, and those stages that can be delegated to support staff.

Activities for the AP

- Manage a significant purchase through the following stages:
  - o Identification of the need for the purchase, with links to the school plan
  - o Establishment of goals for and an evaluation process of the purchase, if appropriate
  - o Management of a decision-making process to identify product/vendor
  - o Identification of a funding source
  - o Management of the purchase order/contracting process

- Identify a project or program area in which you will have budget management responsibility. Reach agreement with your principal on the authority you will possess, the goals you are to pursue, and a process for reviewing progress. Complete the *Budget Management Worksheet* and discuss it with your principal.

Tools

- Budget Management Worksheet

Budget Management Worksheet

Project/program name:

Program goal(s):

Primary evaluation criteria:

Planning document and links to school goals and plan:

Process for project/program and budget planning:

Who has operational decision-making authority?

Budget process timeline:

- Plan and budget development
- Plan and budget adoption and approval
- Hiring and major expenditures
- Budget monitoring
- Fiscal close and program evaluation

What percentage of the budget is devoted to

- Personnel costs
- Materials and supplies
- Release time and consultants
- Other expenditures

What support will you need in managing this project/program?
Who will provide it?

ENROLLMENT PROJECTIONS

Background

One of the principal's most important jobs is to make accurate student enrollment projections. Staffing is based on projected enrollment. Inaccurate projections make for problematic staffing and scheduling, which makes for disruptions of instruction. The last thing any student, teacher, or principal wants to have to do is to reshuffle classes after the start of the school year.

In most school districts, staffing levels are driven by business managers who make their decisions based on financial considerations rather than educational impact. District business offices are likely to make conservative enrollment estimates and are often not particularly sensitive to the impact of adding or removing teaching positions after the start of the school year. For this reason, in most districts it is critically important that principals develop independent enrollment projections based on accurate data and advocate for appropriate staffing when the district and the principal's projections differ.

On the surface, building an enrollment projection would seem to be a simple task: how many in, how many out? At the middle and high school levels this means knowing the number of students graduating from feeder schools and where they will enroll. Maintaining records for at least five years is important, especially for schools that have multiple feeder schools and where feeder schools send students to more than one school, or where competition with charter and private schools is an issue. One also needs to be able to project the number of students who will leave the school to transfer to other schools or drop out.

For elementary schools the matter is more complicated because of the difficulty of projecting kindergarten enrollment. One needs data for several years regarding feeder preschools and knowledge of the percent of your entering students who will have attended a preschool or not. One also needs projections for new housing units in the attendance area.

The development of enrollment projections is an example of a managerial task that is not all that romantic, and that falls outside of what most of us would define as "instructional leadership," yet it is a responsibility that can heavily impact teachers and students. We suggest that assistant principals would be well served by having experience in this area.

Discussion Questions

- What is the history of your enrollment, your internal projections, district projections, and enrollment-driven staffing over the past five years?
- What trends can you see headed your way in the area of enrollment? How can you advocate for your interests with the district?

Shared Activities

- Develop enrollment projection spreadsheets that factor in the appropriate data, taking the *Enrollment Projection Considerations Worksheet* into account.

Activities for the AP

- By the middle of the school year, schedule appointments in feeder schools with administrators, teachers, and students for the purpose of assessing the numbers and the needs of the students who are headed your way.
- Explore unconventional ways of predicting enrollment, such as determining projected housing starts based on county or city data or kindergarten enrollments based upon birth records.

Tools

- Enrollment Projection Considerations Worksheet

Enrollment Projection Considerations Worksheet

Enrollment Projection for Incoming Class, Middle and High School

- Name of feeder schools
- Number of students enrolled in their highest grade for each of the last five years
- Number of students who enrolled at your school from that feeder school for each of the last five years
- Percent of the graduating class from each feeder school that enrolled at your school
- Projection of number of students from each feeder school who will enroll at your school next fall
- Number of new students to the community by grade who enrolled at your school in the summer for each of the last five years

Enrollment Projections for Incoming Class, Elementary School

- Name of feeder preschools
- Number of students coming from each of those preschools for the last five years
- Any enrollment changes at those preschools for the current year that might impact enrollment at your school
- Percent of kindergarteners who did not attend preschool for the last five years
- Location of new housing developments in your community and projected enrollment impact on your school
- Any employment changes in your community that will impact enrollment (e.g., layoffs, relocations, new hiring of major employers)

Enrollment Projection for Returning Students

- Number of students enrolled by grade on March 1 for each of the last five years
- Number of students by grade who returned the following fall for each of the last five years
- Record the increase or decrease by grade for each year

BUILDING THE MASTER SCHEDULE

Background

There is no task that more clearly indicates the underlying values of the school's leadership team than the process of building a master schedule. Each of these questions reflects on the leadership and mission of the school: Is the master schedule designed to satisfy the adults in the building or to meet the needs of the students? Who has primary responsibility for building the master schedule? How engaged is the principal? How collaborative is the process? Is the master schedule built during the teachers' work year or over the summer? What specific classes are placed into the schedule first? Which classes are allowed a small enrollment and which are not? Which student groups are generally in large classes and which are in smaller classes? How much does athletics influence the master schedule? Do teachers who coach an athletic team receive an additional prep period and/or last period prep? Who teaches which students? Are there teachers who only teach advanced classes? Are there teachers who only teach "remedial" classes? Do your strongest teachers teach your most challenging and needy students? Do new teachers receive the toughest assignments or assignments that will nurture their growth as professionals and their success with their students?

**SAMPLE CORE GUIDELINES, VALUES, AND PRIORITIES
FOR MASTER SCHEDULE DEVELOPMENT**

- Our master schedule is designed to meet our students' needs first; adult needs and preferences are a lower priority.

- Our strongest and most experienced teachers take on the most challenging assignments; newer teachers receive assignments they are likely to be most successful with.

- Our schedule is designed to avoid internal segregation of students.

- Remedial classes are first priority for lower class size.

- Our schedule is designed to facilitate teacher collaboration.

We have seen situations in which the principal remains "hands off" in developing the master schedule, leaving the job to assistant principals or counselors. In other cases, we have seen principals hold the schedule close to the vest, controlling the process and denying assistants the opportunity to learn this critical process. We suggest that you make the construction of the master schedule an explicit, transparent, deliberate, and collaborative process, and that principals, assistant principals, counselors, and interested teachers should understand and participate in that process.

You need accurate data in order to build a strong master schedule. What does history tell us is the relationship between spring requests and what we are likely to need in the fall? Which students have not turned in their class requests? Who will complete which courses in summer school?

What classes will new students need? Who will not return? How does student enrollment in particular classes change during the first month of school due to the need to place students in more appropriate classes? These questions can be answered in a timely and accurate manner if one takes the time to use data collected over several years. These data should be explicit, and should not rely on any one person's historic experiences.

Discussion Questions

- If an outsider were to analyze your current master schedule, what values and priorities would he or she say it reflects? What values, priorities, assumptions, and processes should drive the development of your master schedule?
- What has been the history of schedule development and implementation at your building over the past few years? What lessons can you extract from that history?

Shared Activities

- Develop a document that outlines the core values, priorities, and assumptions that will drive your master schedule development process. Get staff input and share the document widely.
- Develop and disseminate a timeline for the master scheduling process that assigns clear roles and responsibilities.
- Build the master schedule together, walking through each step of the process in a deliberate and transparent way.

Activities for the AP

- Identify several successful schools comparable in size to your own. Visit them and learn about their master schedules, their schedule development process, and other lessons you might be able to take back to your own school.
- Work with staff to build a written timeline and task analysis of the scheduling process. Make sure that you have experience with and understand every key step of the process.

Additional Resources

Neubig, M. (2007). *The practitioners guide to scheduling for SLCs and career academies: Equity in action.* Carlsbad, CA: Hudson Publishing.

WORKING WITH PEOPLE

The leaders who work most effectively, it seems to me, never say "I." And that's not because they have trained themselves not to say "I." They don't think "I." They think "we"; they think "team." They understand their job to be to make the team function. They accept responsibility and don't sidestep it, but "we" gets the credit. . . . This is what creates trust, what enables you to get the task done.

—Peter Drucker

A good group is better than a spectacular group. When leaders become superstars, the teacher outshines the teaching. The wise leader settles for good work and lets others have the floor.

—John Heider, *The Tao of Leadership*, 1985

In Part I, we provided some scaffolding to help you build your leadership team and your coaching relationships. In Part II, we provided you with tools to develop your basic management skills and processes, and to focus your conversations on some of the important management responsibilities that are held by school administrators. In this part, we turn your attention a bit more outward, to some of the basics about working with people.

SCHOOL CULTURE AND CLIMATE

Background

There is no shortage of evidence that a positive school culture and climate are prerequisite to and an essential element of school effectiveness. McREL places "building and maintaining a culture in which a common language is employed, ideas are shared, and staff members operate within the norms of cooperation" as second on its list of twenty-one school leadership responsibilities (p. 46).

The words *culture* and *climate* are often used interchangeably, but they are in fact different and related concepts. Climate speaks to the emotional tone of a campus: the morale and feeling state of students and staff. Culture speaks to behaviors: "how we do things around here." Kent Peterson (1994) calls culture "a complex web of norms, values, beliefs and assumptions, traditions and rituals that have built over time as teachers, students, parents, and administrators . . . develop unstated expectations for interacting and working together" (p. 1). Culture and climate are interwoven with all aspects of a school's existence, and while there is probably not much to be gained by a "chicken or egg" discussion (which comes first, a successful school or a positive climate?), it is important to recognize that leaders shape the cultures and climates of their schools. As school leaders, you are the single strongest influence on your school's culture and climate. Effective leaders are strategic and deliberate in building and using climate and culture as leverage points for school improvement.

In several studies of urban school reform, Anthony Bryk has identified what he calls *relational trust* as the best predictor of sustained school improvement (Bryk & Schneider, 2002). Relational trust is defined as being built on four factors: respect, competence, personal regard, and integrity. These factors are closely tied to school culture and climate. Respect and personal regard speak to the quality of relationships within the school community. In trusting school communities, competence is expected and incompetence is not tolerated, and, in exercising integrity, children's interests are put first and people follow through on their commitments.

Marty Krovetz (2008) suggests that in healthy school cultures, students and staff are known and valued as individuals. The school community is infused with high expectations and with the support systems that will allow those expectations to be met.

As principal and assistant principal, you should be brutally honest in assessing the culture and climate of your school. You should recognize that the relationship between the two of you might serve as a tacit model with ripple effects across your school culture. You should understand that both as individuals and as a leadership team, you must deal with school culture, climate, and issues of trust.

Discussion Questions

- How would you characterize culture, climate, and relational trust at your site? How would your staff, students, and community do the same? Little green men from outer space? What specific evidence would support these assessments?
- What kind of model is your relationship as a leadership team for culture, climate, and relationship trust? How can you improve your relationship, and leverage that relationship to help to shape your school?
- Who are the key players in shaping your school's culture? Who socializes new staff, and lets people know "how things are around here?" Who are your storytellers, and what stories are told?
- What are your explicit and tacit traditions, rituals, and norms? Which are productive, which are counterproductive? To what degree do you walk your talk, particularly around maintaining high expectations of staff? How can you intervene to build a more positive, collaborative, and productive culture?

Shared Activities

- Survey staff, students, and community about school culture and climate.
- Conduct student and community focus groups about school culture and climate

Activities for the AP

- Shadow a student for a full day to get a student's eye view of the school's culture.
- Identify some key "symbolic leadership" roles at your site and take responsibility for them. This might include presiding over student or staff recognition events or other celebrations, or orienting new students or staff.

Additional Resources

Deal, T., & Peterson, K. (1999). *Shaping school culture: The heart of leadership.* San Francisco: Jossey-Bass.

Krovetz, M. (2008). *Fostering resilience: Expecting all students to use their minds and hearts well.* Thousand Oaks, CA: Corwin Press.

Tools

- School Culture Survey

School Culture Survey

Directions

Rate each norm/value on the following scale:

1 = Almost always characteristic of our school

2 = Generally characteristic of our school

3 = Seldom characteristic of our school

4 = Not characteristic

For each norm/value, please provide a recent illustrative example of how that norm is demonstrated through individual or organizational behavior.

Norm/Value	Rating	Recent Illustrative Example
1. Moral Purpose: The school community is driven by a commitment to make a positive difference in the lives of students and their community.		
2. Professional Learning Community: Commitment to examining practice with a focus on improving student achievement.		
3. Experimentation: Ongoing professional development with an interest in trying new practices and evaluating the results.		
4. High Expectations: A pervasive push for high standards-based performance for students and all staff, using multiple data sources to inform assessments and personnel processes.		
5. Public Service: Staff understands that their role is to serve the community. Staff respects and honors community values, culture, and contributions.		
6. Trust and Confidence: A pervasive feeling that people will do what's right between and across groups. There is no "us v. them."		
7. Support for Personal and Professional Growth: Individual coaching and mentoring are pervasive.		
8. Tangible Support: Financial and material assistance are aligned to the goals determined within a cycle of continuous improvement. People have what they need to do their work.		
9. Reaching Out to the Knowledge Base: Use of research, reading of professional journals, attending workshops.		

Norm/Value	Rating	Recent Illustrative Example
10. Appreciation and Recognition: Acknowledgment of quality student and faculty work and effort.		
11. Caring, Celebration, Humor: There is a sense of community with shared purpose and joy. Personal balance and health are values.		
12. Appreciation of Leadership: Specifically, leadership provided by teachers, principals, and other professional staff.		
13. Clarity of Goals and Outcomes: There is a coherent vision and action plan tied to measurable goals that members of the community could articulate and relate to their own work.		
14. Protection of What's Important: School goals, priorities, and core cultural values.		
15. Involvement of Stakeholders in Decision Making: Those who will be affected by decisions are involved in making them; diverse points of view are included and honored.		
16. Traditions: Rituals and events that celebrate and support core school and community values.		
17. Honest, Open Communication: Teaching and learning is public practice with multiple opportunities for peer and administrative observation and feedback. Coaching and feedback are valued among all practitioners.		
18. Willingness to Confront the "Brutal Facts": A pervasive culture in which multiple data sources are used to expose student achievement gaps as well as gaps in instructional expertise, within the context of fostering "critical friendships."		

SOURCE: Adapted from the New Teacher Center at University of California, Santa Cruz.

RECOGNITION

Background

How we recognize teachers, staff, parents, and students indicates a lot about our values and how vision guides our actions. People watch where and with whom leaders spend their time and resources and assume that these actions demonstrate what that leader thinks is most important. If a school's vision statement stresses cooperation, problem solving, and critical thinking, but the school recognizes a "student of the month" and "an employee of the month," the practice may tell others that you value individual accomplishment over cooperation. If faculty meetings dominated by information-giving provide teachers with little opportunity for real input, the message is that you do not value collaboration. If teachers are praised for having their objectives posted on the board, but not acknowledged for engaging their students in critical thinking, you are sending a mixed message.

School leaders have little opportunity to recognize employees with money, and financial rewards may be among the least powerful they can offer. However, you do have access to resources that are highly valued by your teachers, classified staff, students, and parents. Think about the following:

- How you talk with people indicates a lot about who and what you value. The more you talk with teachers about best practice and meeting the needs of specific students, the more teachers feel valued as professionals.
- When you use meeting time for collaborative decision making and quality professional development, teachers know that you value them as professionals.
- When you build your master schedule, who teaches what and when indicates your values. The same is true in elementary schools when student are assigned to classes for the following year. Are these decisions made to meet students' needs, or based on seniority, tradition, or political pull?
- Assuring that your classroom observations, formal and informal, are used to improve teaching practice rather than fulfilling the obligations of the contract or to catch people making mistakes, demonstrates that you value and recognize effective teaching.
- The more collaboratively you develop the school budget, the more you indicate to teachers, classified staff, parents, and students that you value their ideas and insights.
- The more you build in rewards and recognition for the majority of students who work to be successful in school, the clearer your commitment is to the learning of all students.

Probably the best way to recognize people is to say hello to them each day. No staff member should go two consecutive days without you talking with him or her. Knowing the names of teachers, staff, students, and parents and using their names regularly in greetings with a smile builds a culture where people feel valued. When you do give people feedback, it should be as specific as possible. Saying something like "great lesson" to a teacher provides a warm, fuzzy, but not particularly powerful pat on the back. Telling that same teacher, "I loved the way you checked for understanding with white boards, and the scaffolding you provided your English language learners," provides specific reinforcement for specific teaching strategies, and lets teachers know what you are looking for when you visit classrooms.

In a traditional school environment, the principal is the father and mother figure. Recognition and rewards flow from him or her. In the spirit of developing leadership in assistant principals and building distributed leadership across the school, you should find ways to ensure that the principal is not the sole font of recognition and rewards.

Discussion Questions

- What do people say about what you value? What specific evidence do they supply?
- What formal and informal structures are in place for recognizing and rewarding various members of your school community in a manner that is consistent with your vision and values? What evidence do you have that rewards are numerous, noticed, and valued?

Shared Activities

- Keep a daily journal of how you reward and recognize people at school for a week. Who is on this list? Who is not? What can you do to broaden the number of people included.
- Share responsibilities in leading some or all of the activities outlined on the *Three Recognition Strategies Worksheet*.

Activities for the AP

- Pick three teachers, three classified staff, three parents, and three students. Develop and implement a process to regularly recognize their contributions.

Tools

- Three Recognition Strategies Worksheet

Three Recognition Strategies Worksheet

A Simple Method for Recognizing Student Contributions

Every student fills out three 5 x 7 cards in each class, addressing one side to their parents, and writing on the other side, "Dear Mom and Dad, My teacher wants you to know that I have been successful at *** in *** class and am learning a lot about ***. Love, ***." Teachers alphabetize the cards and once a week sends home five cards. The intent is for all cards to be mailed home over a four-month period. The process will take teachers no more than five minutes a week. The payoff in terms of positive feelings by parents and in student motivation will be very large.

Learning Which Students Are Known Well and Which Are Not

On chart paper, post the names of all students in the school in alphabetical order. Give teachers red stick-um dots. Give classified staff green stick-um dots. Teachers and classified staff place a dot next to the name of any student they know by name and know something about first hand apart from the classroom. Who has lots of red dots? Who has lots of green dots? Who has none or few? What does this say about the culture of your school? Develop a plan with teachers and classified staff for how to know better those students with few dots.

Learning Which Staff Members You Interact With

Make a list of all teachers and classified staff members. Over a week place a checkmark by the name of each person you talk with about teaching and learning, including specific student behavior. Who has lots of checkmarks? Who has few? What does this say about how you interact with staff? What will you do to increase the number of checkmarks? Repeat this on a monthly basis in order to monitor how well you are doing.

CLASSIFIED STAFF

Background

Who at your school is the most invested in the success of your students? Very often it is classified staff. They live in the community. They know many community members. They are most likely to be representative of your community. Their children and grandchildren attend your schools. They are long-term members of your staff. They deserve your respect. Their contributions, voice, and individual and group potential must be honored.

Classified staff members often report that they are neglected and taken for granted. They are not turned to for input, nor offered opportunities for professional development. In relating to administrators, they may quickly size up those that relate well to classified staff, and those that do not. The administrator universally condemned by his classified staff is not long for the job.

As an important step in building a leadership team and in shaping your school's culture, we suggest that you engage in a deliberate process of getting to know your classified staff, and of soliciting their input around school and community issues.

Discussion Questions

- Who are the classified staff at your school? Use the *Classified Staff Worksheet* to guide discussion.
- What do you do to include your classified staff in your school's learning community?
- How do you and the classified staff members assess their skills and areas for growth and offer them professional development?

Shared Activities

- Develop a plan for regular communication with classified staff, including regular meetings for the purpose of soliciting classified staff members' ideas and input.
- Take a few weeks, and through informal contacts, gather the data for the *Classified Staff Worksheet* that you were unable to produce in your internal discussion.
- Use the *Classified Staff Satisfaction Survey* to assess perceptions of your classified staff.

Activities for the AP

- Take responsibility for supervising a group of classified staff (e.g., campus supervisors, custodial staff, office staff.) As part of the supervision process, meet regularly with the group and individuals

to problem solve. Work with the group to develop individual and
mutual leadership capacity.

- Take the time to build informal relationships with classified staff
members. Target individuals and groups you would be least likely
to interact with if you did not make deliberate efforts.

Tools

- Classified Staff Worksheet
- Classified Staff Satisfaction Survey

Classified Staff Worksheet

Getting to know your people . . .		Gender	Ethnicity	Years at Site	Graduated From Site?	Lives in District?	Kids, Grandkids in Schools?	Other Interests of Note
Name	**Position**							

Classified Staff Satisfaction Survey

What is your job classification?
_____

On a 1 to 4 continuum, please answer the following questions.
1 = highly satisfied, 2 = satisfied, 3 = not satisfied, 4 = highly dissatisfied

_____ 1. I am treated respectfully by other classified staff.

_____ 2. I am treated respectfully by my supervisor.

_____ 3. I am treated respectfully by teachers.

_____ 4. I am treated respectfully by students.

_____ 5. I am treated respectfully by parents.

_____ 6. Classified staff work well together.

_____ 7. I am asked for my opinion about issues related to my job.

_____ 8. I am asked for my opinion about school and student issues.

_____ 9. There are opportunities for me to grow on the job.

_____ 10. I have input in defining my job responsibilities.

_____ 11. I have the opportunity to be formally involved in school governance.

_____ 12. I like coming to work.

_____ 13. I feel that I am an important member of the school community.

_____ 14. I receive timely, helpful, and fair supervision.

_____ 15. All staff at this school is held to high standards of performance.

_____ 16. I am proud to be a member of this school's staff.

Comments:

DIFFICULT CONVERSATIONS

Background

We are in education because we care about people. We're altruistic. We don't enjoy having difficult conversations with subordinates, and many of us avoid difficult conversations most of the time. We may even be uncomfortable with the word "subordinate," which implies a pecking order or a command and control structure. Nonetheless, we are responsible for the staff and students at our sites, and those individuals look to us for feedback, guidance, and limits. Effective leaders have to be willing and able to have uncomfortable, difficult, frank conversations.

It is not unusual for principals and assistant principals to be responsible for supervising staff members many years older than themselves, often individuals with much longer histories and deeper relationships at their sites. Every one of us in leadership positions has had to have difficult conversations with staff members around issues of job performance, personal hygiene, communication style, and so forth. We have had to dismiss people we like and/or have deep empathy for.

Research demonstrates that one of the most demotivating, morale sapping things a leader can do is to tolerate or ignore unsatisfactory performance. Committed staff members reason, "I'm working my tush off and Jones down the hall has been getting away with murder for years. . . . Why should I care if the boss doesn't?" You need to deal with the Joneses.

Because having difficult conversations is so difficult for many of us, they should be planned and practiced. Principals should share the wealth, asking assistant principals to conduct these sorts of conversations with scaffolding and support.

Discussion Questions

- As a leadership team, what is your history around difficult conversations? What issues have you avoided, and which have you taken on?

Shared Activities

- Identify a problem situation that centers around an individual that you have collectively avoided dealing with. Develop an action plan to deal with the problem and touch base on your progress at your regular meetings.

Activities for the AP

- Identify a supervisory situation in which you need to have a difficult conversation. Use the *Planning Difficult Conversations Worksheet* to plan the interaction. If possible, have your principal or a colleague observe the conversation and provide you with feedback. If the situation is a personnel issue that should be documented, work with your principal and/or human resources staff to take appropriate steps.

Tools

• Planning Difficult Conversations Worksheet

Planning Difficult Conversations Worksheet

Basic Considerations

- Difficult conversations need to take place at an appropriate time and place.
- Focus on professional expectations and behaviors, not on the individual's nature.
- Acknowledge emotions, but do not dwell on them; do not allow the conversation to be hijacked by defensiveness, avoidance, or accusation.
- Focus on impacts on students and colleagues, not on you.
- Focus on evidence and data, not your personal opinions.
- Produce clear next steps and an accountability plan.

Planning the Conversation

- What is your concern?
- What data do you have to substantiate the concern?
- What has been the impact of the concern on students and/or staff?
- What, specifically, must change in order to address the concern?
- What specific outcome do you want to produce, including a timeline, your support role, and accountability process?

Conducting the Conversation

- Open the conversation and label it as serious.
- Acknowledge that it may be difficult for the individual and that you assume that the individual has the school's best interests at heart. It is not about the individual as a person, but about professional standards and practice.
- Share your concern and supporting evidence.
- Explain your expectations for satisfactory performance based on institutional standards.
- Allow the individual to react; listen, but do not allow the conversation to be derailed.
- Ask how the concern could be addressed. Try to arrive at a mutually agreeable action plan.
- Outline an action plan that includes a timeline, accountability, and the role that you or others will play in supporting the individual.
- Ask the individual for feedback about the conversation.
- If appropriate, follow up the conversation with a written summary within twenty-four hours.

EFFECTIVE MEETINGS

Background

When you were in elementary school and were asked what you wanted to do when you grew up, did you answer, "Go to meetings"? We doubt it. Few of us relish attending meetings, and many of us dread them. This is often because they are poorly facilitated and unproductive. School leadership teams need to ensure that their meetings are conducted well, and assistant principals should become masters of meeting design and facilitation.

Schools are complex and (ideally) democratic organizations where we spend a tremendous amount of time communicating, deciding, and coordinating our shared work. Collaborative leadership improves the quality of decision making and, when the decisions are focused on students, improves the quality of teaching and learning. When meetings are managed well, participants understand that their time is respected and that leadership has a genuine interest in collaboration. In effective meetings participants feel engaged and they feel that their voices are valued. At schools where meetings are poorly run, teachers are more likely to keep their classroom door closed and to continue private practice. The quality of meetings at your site, those that you facilitate and those that you do not, says a tremendous amount about the effectiveness of your leadership team.

Teachers let us know when they don't value our meetings. They read student papers, they read the newspaper, they hold side conversations, and they walk out whispering in small groups. These behaviors may be rude, but they are also often an accurate reflection of the quality of the meetings. Too many meetings consist of information dumps, wandering discussions, and unclear decisions with little follow up or accountability.

Most of us know how to conduct effective meetings, but we get sloppy. Despite their importance, meetings are often planned carelessly and at the last minute. Any time you facilitate a meeting, you have an opportunity and responsibility to model good teaching and your expectations and values. Like a good lesson, an effective meeting is well planned, interactive, and produces measurable outcomes. In a school where shared leadership is valued, meeting design and facilitation are shared.

What are the characteristics of productive meetings?

- There are established norms that are revisited and monitored at every meeting.
- Agendas are collaboratively set and in people's hands at least twenty-four hours in advance.
- They start on time and end on time.
- They have clear purposes and goals.
- They are interactive, seeking input from participants and utilizing well-planned protocols.
- They are well facilitated to ensure participation and focus on the agenda; tangential items are recorded, but do not divert the meeting.
- An action plan is developed for all action items.

- Decision-making protocols are planned in advance and are explicit to participants, building consensus and buy-in.
- There are assigned roles: facilitator, recorder, timekeeper, norm processor, content processor.
- The right people are in attendance.

Model effective meetings with your leadership team. Train, support, and monitor others at your site, including department and grade-level chairs, as they facilitate meetings. Bad meetings are endemic in our K–12 schools, and they are expensive, both in terms of staff time and their impact on school culture.

Leading productive meetings is a habit of mind. Meeting planning is a backward-design process, beginning with clarity about desired outcomes. Assume that it takes approximately an hour of planning for every hour of meeting time. Make it one of your goals as a leadership team to improve the quality of meetings across your site. Share responsibility for facilitating meetings, and give one another direct feedback and support.

Discussion Questions

- Evaluate a recent staff, grade-level, or department meeting in light of the characteristics listed above.
- Targeting a particular regular meeting at your site, what are some specific steps you can take to make improvements?

Shared Activities

- Plan the next staff meeting together. Use a backward-planning process. Share facilitation responsibilities and provide one another with feedback. Anticipate individuals who might be difficult at the meeting and develop a strategy for dealing with them.
- Work with department and grade-level chairs to help them plan effective meetings, monitor the meetings, and provide feedback.

Activities for the AP

- Plan and facilitate parts of a staff or grade-level meeting.
- Conduct a meeting facilitation workshop for teacher leaders and/or parents, students, and classified leaders.

Additional Resources

Morley, C. (1994). *How to get the most out of meetings*. Alexandria VA: Association for Supervision and Curriculum Development.

Tools

- Sample Meeting Planning and Agenda Format Worksheet

Sample Meeting Planning and Agenda Format Worksheet

Meeting Type:				Date:		Time:
Planned and Convened By:						
Facilitator:		Timekeeper:		Recorder:		
Meeting Norms:						

Meeting Norms:
- ·
- ·
- ·
- ·
- ·

Agenda Item	Time	Desired Outcome	Decision/Next Steps	Person Responsible	Timeline	Deliverable

DECISION MAKING AND PROBLEM SOLVING

Background

As your school's leadership team, you are charged with solving problems and making and following through on decisions. Are you proactive in identifying and tackling problems, or are you a crisis-driven organization? Are you deliberate in your decision-making processes, or are decisions made in a seemingly random way? Do you revisit the problems you have addressed and the decisions you have made in the spirit of continuous improvement, or is an issue gone forever once it has slipped from the foreground?

As school administrators you make hundreds of decisions a day that range from the mundane to the strategic. You negotiate a universe in which today's seemingly trivial decision could lead to tomorrow's lawsuit or headline. Your leadership team will be more effective and efficient if you take the time to be deliberate and explicit in your decision-making processes, and your assistant principal will be a more confident and better leader if he or she has had responsibility for high-stakes decision making. You will be called upon to make fewer decisions, and the decisions you make will be better and more consistent, if you are proactive in identifying problems and in setting up systems to prevent their recurrence.

Decision making can be described as having three stages: planning, deciding, and implementing. At the planning stage, we outline who participates in the making of which decisions. We clarify and communicate the types of decision-making processes that will be applied to types of decisions; will a decision be made unilaterally, with input, by consensus, or through a vote? We are explicit about the values that drive our decision making, and the metrics by which we will evaluate our decisions.

At the deciding stage, we gather data to inform the process and we appropriately consult and/or involve the individuals who will be affected by the decision. We make a decision in a manner that is consistent with the process that was communicated in the planning stage. We use well-planned protocols, and facilitate the process in a manner that is likely to build consensus and buy in. We communicate the decision, timeline, individuals responsible for implementation, and the process by which the decision's implementation will be monitored, evaluated, and adjusted.

At the implementation state, the appropriate individuals carry out their responsibilities in a manner that is consistent with the decision, and leadership ensures that implementation is monitored, evaluated, and adjusted, and that appropriate groups are updated regarding the implementation.

This simple process often breaks down. Our experience suggests that there are several ways in which decision making flounders in schools. The first is when the decision-making process is not clear from the get-go. This happens when a principal leads an assistant principal to believe he has authority to make a decision, and then reverses the AP's decision, or when a principal leads a faculty to believe that it will make a decision that the principal intends to make herself. Another typical scenario is the leadership team that avoids making a clear decision, and the problem or issue surfaces again and again in a reenactment of *Groundhog Day*. A last, typical, and deadly dysfunction is the leadership team that fails to follow through on decisions to ensure they are implemented and evaluated.

Many of the decisions we make in schools, and certainly the decisions that fall into the "urgent" category, are driven by problems. One test of your effectiveness as a leadership team is the degree to which you are proactive in problem solving. It is always interesting to talk with staff members about the kinds of problems that drive them crazy. Most have their roots in systems issues. Examples include how parents drop off and pick up students, the way students are guided through the cafeteria line, substitute teacher procedures, how attendance is picked up, how student discipline is dealt with, how use of the intercom is monitored, and how textbooks are collected and given to students. Many of these simple systems problems generate traffic for administrators; daily interruptions and requests for low-stakes decisions that keep administrators out of classrooms and away from engagement with instruction. Developing an effective system to deal with any of these issues makes the school run more smoothly, positively affects staff morale, and improves teaching and learning.

Discussion Questions

- How have you been doing as a team regarding decision making? What are your decision-making processes and authority? Do you feel backed up in the decisions that you make? How well does your team follow through on its decisions?
- Review the process and outcome for implementing a recent group decision that was primarily the responsibility of the assistant principal to implement. How effective do you feel the implementation has been? How do you know? Are you both aware of the implementation? How would you change the process and outcome?
- What is an example of a problem that irritates staff and puts low-stakes decisions on your plate? How could it be resolved using a systems approach?

Shared Activities

- Identify some typical decisions made by you as individuals, a team, and a staff; complete and discuss the *Decision-Making Matrix Worksheet*. Make sure you are very clear about the AP's decision-making authority.

Activities for the AP

- Take responsibility for planning and leading a decision-making process around a high-stakes issue that will involve many stakeholders.
- Use the worksheet *Protocol for Preparing to Solve Typical School Problems Worksheet* to guide you in leading a process to tackle a systems issue at your school.

Additional Resources

McDonald, J. (2007). *The power of protocols: An educator's guide to better practice.* New York: Teachers College Press.

Ohle, N., & Morley, C. (1994). *How to solve typical school problems.* Alexandria, VA: Association for Supervision and Curriculum Development.

Tools

- Decision-Making Matrix Worksheet
- Protocol for Preparing to Solve Typical School Problems Worksheet

Decision-Making Matrix Worksheet

Who decides what, and how does the decision get made?

Type of Decision	Lead Decision Maker	Others to Be Involved	Unilateral by Decision Maker	Final by Decision	Consensus of Specified Group	Majority of Specified Group	Other

Protocol for Preparing to Solve
Typical School Problems Worksheet

Background

Make a clear case that the issue is important and worth dealing with. Understand the reasons why this issue is bothering people. What data do you have? Who has a stake in the solution to this issue? Who has a stake in the situation remaining unchanged?

Problem (one sentence)

The problem is that . . .

Purpose (one sentence)

The purpose of addressing this problem is to . . .

Questions

What are the key questions that need to be addressed?

Who has a stake in solving this problem? Who has a stake in the status quo?

Your intervention

Very specifically, how will you engage others in deciding on an action plan?

How will you implement that action plan?

Evaluation

How will you evaluate the effectiveness of the intervention?

What did you learn?

COMMUNICATIONS
AND PUBLIC INFORMATION

Communication pathways are the veins and arteries of new ideas.
—Kouzes & Pozner, 1992

Background

In this world of spam, bumper stickers, and podcasts, it can be hard for school leaders to get their message across. We believe that your school should have a clear strategy for formal communications; a variety of mechanisms for getting the word out, and planned procedures for responding to press inquiries. Assistant principals need to be part of the communications team, gaining experience in this realm, and contributing to the school's public information process.

The following are some of the characteristics of effective formal written internal communications (such as weekly staff bulletins):

- They are released on a regular basis, predictably and reliably.
- They consolidate announcements and other information in one place in order to reduce or eliminate other communications.
- They explicitly convey and reinforce the school's vision, expectations, and progress.
- There is a clear expectation that they will be read by appropriate staff, and time is not wasted in staff meetings repeating information that has been conveyed in writing.
- They celebrate the successes of individuals, of the school community, and its students.
- They model high standards for form, content, and brevity.

Written communications with the community should reflect most of the above, and should address the following concerns as well:

- They should be in a language and writing style that is accessible to the parent community.
- They should be delivered to the community in a manner that it is likely to reach it, probably through a variety of means. Any one medium (e.g., newsletters, newspapers, the Web) is likely to reach only a small percentage of your target group.

In our experience, many schools waste a tremendous amount of time and energy on ineffective communications, and their leaders are frustrated when tactics they know won't work . . . don't. If sending a note home with students to announce open house the day before the event didn't produce a good turnout, don't blame the parents; try another tactic.

Working with the news media is a related and critically important skill. Assistant principals should be given the opportunity to interact with the media, but only after some discussion and role-play practice in working with them. Always debrief, and remember to bring the district office into the loop when appropriate.

Discussion Questions

- How do your internal and external communications rate against the criteria outlined above and against your aspirations for your school?
- Who are your most important audiences and what communication strategies might be most effective in reaching them?

Shared Activities

- Chart the formal internal and external communication mechanisms you currently have in place. Are there gaps and/or redundancies? How can you strengthen your school's communications, but at the same time reduce your own workload?
- Develop schoolwide norms for the use of e-mail in an effort to improve communications and decrease excess e-mail traffic.
- Develop a media plan and share it with staff. Role-play reporter interviews with one another before you return the reporter's phone call.
- On a monthly basis, identify a positive story to pitch to the media. Write a press release or call a local reporter with the lead.

Activities for the AP

- Randomly select the names of ten parents. Call each of them and interview them about where they get information about the school and how you could improve your reach into the parent community.
- For a defined period, take responsibility for writing staff and/or parent newsletters. Include commentary or reflections with your byline.
- Take responsibility for gathering positive school stories to share with the media, and draft press releases to get them out into the world.
- When an appropriate breaking story occurs, serve as the site spokesperson with the principal's agreement and coaching.

Additional Resources

Northwest Regional Educational Laboratory. (2001). *The power of public relations in schools.* http://www.nwrel.org/request/feb01/
National School Public Relations Association, http://www.nspra.org

COMMUNITY ENGAGEMENT

Background

In his book, *What Works in Schools: Translating Research Into Action*, Robert Marzano (2003) identifies eleven factors essential to effective school reform. One of these factors is parent and community involvement. Marzano suggests that parent and community involvement includes three elements: communication, participation, and governance. Schools benefit when parents support their programs by being present as volunteers and supporters, when parents and community members have a genuine role in shaping the school's vision and programs, and when there are effective mechanisms for communication between the community and the school.

Effective schools understand their communities and are responsive to their needs, and they take full advantage of the variety of both formal and informal resources that are situated in their communities.

School principals, particularly high school principals, are often ambassadors to the community at large, playing a symbolic leadership role for "flagship" local schools: schools that often are hung with a mantle of tradition.

Principals can help their assistants be successful in the domain of community engagement by providing them with opportunities to get to know their school communities, to engage with those communities, and to lead some of the formal and informal activities that take place in relation to those communities.

Discussion Questions

- What are the formal mechanisms for parent and community involvement at your school? What are the processes through which parents can bring complaints and suggestions, and have a say in decision making?
- What community/cultural groups are you least connected to? How can you get to know these groups, and give them an opportunity to get to know you?
- How are you perceived by various elements in the community? How can the AP help improve the ways in which you are perceived?

Shared Activities

- Make a graphic representation of the community constituencies, public agencies, and key businesses in your district. What insights can you derive from this map? What groups have you neglected, and what opportunities do you see for your school?
- Develop a brief parent involvement handbook that summarizes ways in which parents and community members can engage with the school.

- Agree to hand responsibility for interface with a parent/community governance group to the assistant. Collaboratively plan and develop agendas for meetings and debrief after each session.

Activities for the AP

- Represent the school at community groups such as Rotary, LULAC, NAACP, City Council, and YMCA.
- Immerse yourself in community settings outside of your own cultural comfort zone; attend church services at a new denomination, have coffee "klatches" in community centers or living rooms, and walk your neighborhoods.
- Identify a particular target population, such as affiliates of a local gang. Get to know that population by making home visits, hanging out with them on campus and off, and meeting with the formal and informal leadership of the group, as well as the social services and other public agencies that interface with them.

DEALING WITH DIFFICULT PARENTS

Background

When school administrators reflect on what causes them stress on the job, they almost always talk about dealing with difficult adults. They almost never mention dealing with students. Many of us have said, "If it weren't for the adults, this school would be a great place!" Among the toughest challenges are angry parents. Dealing with such parents is a skill that can be learned, and is often one of the first focus areas for a thoughtful principal/assistant principal coaching relationship.

Most parents see themselves as advocates for their children. They may approach the school with their own child's interests in mind and with little regard for what is best for other students. Others may be frustrated with their child's behavior and not know how to deal with it, and they blame the school for not helping the student learn better behavior. In both cases the perspectives of the parent and the school administrator are different, which may lead to breakdowns in communication and lack of mutual respect.

As a principal/assistant principal team, it is important that you support one another in dealing with parents. We might say that you should convey a "united front," but this implies that it is "you against them." Rather, your goal should be to have clear, shared understandings of the outcomes you wish to produce with parents and work as a team to resolve conflicts.

It is important to always start with the assumption that the parent is doing what he or she thinks is best for the child. It is also important to be appropriately prepared with background information and a game plan prior to meeting with parents. And, remembering our earlier discussion of time management, in dealing with parents you must protect your time for "important, not urgent" instructional leadership responsibilities. An angry parent demanding your immediate attention can be asked to return at an appointment time, and a conversation with a difficult parent can be premised with a statement such as, "We have twenty minutes for this conversation. What do we hope to accomplish?" A well-trained office staff can defuse many situations by gathering background information for you, directing concerns to the right individuals, and scheduling appointments after an aggrieved party has had time to cool off.

Discussion Questions

- Think about several recent interactions with difficult parents. What made these interactions go well? When they did not go well, what could you have done differently?
- What data do you have on how your school is perceived in the community? What cross-cultural issues may be in play when difficult situations arise?

Shared Activities

- Meet with office staff and agree on an explicit strategy for dealing with upset or demanding adults.
- Conduct several conferences with difficult parents together. Take turns leading the conferences. Debrief immediately afterward.

Activities for the AP

- Use the worksheet *Planning Guide for Parent Meetings* to plan and evaluate a difficult parent meeting.
- Lead a survey and/or focus group process to assess parent perceptions of your school and administration. Is your school seen as fair and responsive to parents and students? What issues of race and class impact the ways in which parents interact with your school and its staff?

Tools

- Planning Guide for Parent Meetings

Planning Guide for Parent Meetings

Plan Backward

- What is the background for this meeting?

- What do I hope will be the outcome of this meeting?

- How will I know if this outcome has been attained—short term and long term?

- What information do I need in preparation for this meeting?

- What will I do if the meeting is not going well?

- What do I know about how this parent(s) will approach the meeting and me?

- How can I prepare for this specific parent(s)?

- How much time shall I limit this meeting to?

Evaluation of Parent Conference

- What were my goals for this conference?

- What were the outcomes of this conference? What specific data do I have to support this conclusion?

- What could I have done to be better prepared for this conference?

- What did I do to keep the conference on target?

- How did I use my knowledge of the student in the conference? What specific data do I have that this preparation was effective?

- How did I use my knowledge of the parent(s) in the conference? What specific data do I have that this preparation was effective?

- How could I have been more effective in this conference?

- What feedback did I get from the parent(s) about the conference?

- If a teacher was included in this conference, what feedback did I get from the teacher about the conference?

- Did the conference stay within the time allocated? If not, why not?

INSTRUCTIONAL LEADERSHIP IV

Let us not be content to wait and see what will happen, but give us the determination to make the right things happen.

—Horace Mann

We all signed on to be instructional leaders. We are in this business because we want to make a difference for kids and have a positive impact in classrooms. Yet most administrators complain that they spend less time on instruction than they think they should, and many assistant principals report that they spend almost no time on instructional leadership.

The ISLLC Standards place a strong emphasis on instructional leadership; Standard 2 calls for school leaders who "promote the success of all students by advocating, nurturing, and sustaining a school culture and instructional program conducive to student learning and staff professional growth." McREL's meta-analysis of research on school leadership demonstrates that school administrators have a significant impact on student achievement, and that principals' involvement in monitoring and evaluating instruction; in curriculum, instruction, and assessment; and knowledge of the same are highly correlated with school performance.

If your principal/assistant principal relationship is strong and effective, you spend a large portion of your time focused on instructional issues. If you are building a coaching-based apprenticeship relationship, the assistant principal is taking on instructional responsibilities and is spending a significant portion of his or her time in classrooms, teacher conferences, department meetings, and grappling with student data.

Being an instructional leader doesn't mean you have to know it all. It means you keep the conversation focused on teaching and learning and on a limited number of carefully identified improvement goals. An effective instructional leader asks questions over and over, provides resources including time and accurate data, builds a strong instructional leadership team, models quality teaching practices at every opportunity, spends hours daily in classrooms and in conversations with teachers, and regularly recognizes and rewards the efforts and accomplishments of teachers, students, and parents related to teaching and learning.

The full scope of instructional leadership extends well beyond what we are able to address in this short volume. What we present here are a selection of topic areas and activities that we believe will be fruitful as you focus your principal/assistant principal team on instruction.

PROFESSIONAL READING

Outside of a dog, a book is a man's best friend. Inside of a dog, it's too dark to read.
—Groucho Marx

Background

Professional reading is as much a part of the daily life of strong educational leaders as are classroom visits and conversations with colleagues. We are part of an academic profession, and we have a fundamental obligation to ground our daily work in the history, theory, research, and current thinking in our field. Unfortunately, many of us avoid professional reading both because it's not our favorite thing to do, and because it falls into that "important, not urgent" quadrant in Covey's framework (see Part II on Time Management). We wouldn't think of seeing a doctor who doesn't read professional journals on a regular basis, yet we seem to accept the fact that most educators are not consumers of professional literature.

Principals and assistant principals have the opportunity to improve their practice through professional reading and to model informed practice for their staff. It is one thing to propose an initiative to your staff because you think it is a good idea; it is another when you can support the idea with research and models from the outside world.

As we discuss later in this book, professional learning communities (PLC) can propel school improvement. A school's administrative team, principal, assistant principals, and perhaps others clearly can constitute a professional learning community. And while a PLC should focus its work on improving practice and should not be merely a reading club, a PLC can be a venue for powerful discussions about professional reading and its application at your site.

Discussion Questions

- What have been the most important and influential professional books for each of you?
- What journals and magazines do you regularly read?
- How can you use professional reading at your site to support your school improvement efforts?

Shared Activities

- On a monthly or quarterly basis, identify short readings to be duplicated and shared with staff.
- Select a book or articles to read as a leadership team, and conduct structured discussions of your reading. End the discussions by summarizing implications and action steps for your site.

Activities for the AP

- Read!
- Volunteer to identify reading that will be useful to a school committee or department. Lead a discussion of that reading with the group.

SIX PERIODICALS EVERY SCHOOL LEADER SHOULD READ RELIGIOUSLY

- Your local newspaper

- A national newspaper such as the *New York Times* or *Los Angeles Times*

- *Education Week*

- The Association of Supervision and Curriculum Development's *Educational Leadership*

- Phi Delta Kappa's *Kappan*

- Your professional association's journal such as the American Association of School Administrator's *The School Administrator*

SUPERVISING AND SUPPORTING TEACHERS

*Teacher qualifications, teacher's knowledge and skills, make more difference for
student learning than any other single factor. Clearly that means if we want to
improve student learning, what we have to do is invest in teachers' learning.*

—Linda Darling-Hammond

Background

You know that the single most important factor in your school's success is
what happens on a daily basis in each of your classrooms between your teachers and your students. *Knowing, supervising, and supporting daily instructional
practices in your classrooms must be your single highest priority.* But if your leadership team is like most, your daily routines probably don't reflect that priority.

In previous parts of this book, we have suggested that you work together
on time management. One of the primary goals of your time management
efforts should be to maintain your focus on the "important, not urgent"
work of observing and coaching teachers. We have also suggested that you
should be meeting regularly with one another to collaborate about "important, not urgent" issues related to instruction. One of your most frequent topics of discussion should be what you are observing in classrooms, and how
you are working to help teachers refine their daily instructional practice.

If your district and leadership team are like most around the country,
there is an established formal process for teacher supervision, and you have
divided responsibilities for teacher supervision among the members of your
administrative team. If yours is a typical situation, you struggle to complete
required procedures and paperwork in a timely way, and your teachers don't
get a whole lot out of the process. In most schools, teacher supervision is seen
as something to be gotten out of the way—not as the powerful tool it should be.

Charlotte Danielson (2000) suggests that teacher supervision has two fundamental purposes: nurturing professional growth and ensuring teaching
quality. As supervisors, then, you have two responsibilities: ensuring that
every one of your teachers meets professional standards and helping each of
your teachers grow in their professional practices. We often fail at both responsibilities, allowing weak teachers to receive tenure, tenured veterans to continue as employees even as they fail to meet professional standards, and
neglecting the potential growth of our already satisfactory staff members.

Effective supervision has both *formative* and *summative* elements. It
requires ongoing engagement with teachers, and the use of data from a variety
of sources. It requires that you focus not only on teacher behaviors, but also on
student behaviors and evidence of student achievement. The following
graphic, developed by the New Teacher Center, represents the formative and
summative nature of the formal supervision process when done well.

Throughout this process you want to establish the same kind of coaching relationship between administrator and teacher that we talked about
establishing in Part I of this book between principal and assistant principal.
The coaching language we outline in Part II is as helpful in working with
your supervisees as it is in your principal/assistant principal relationship.

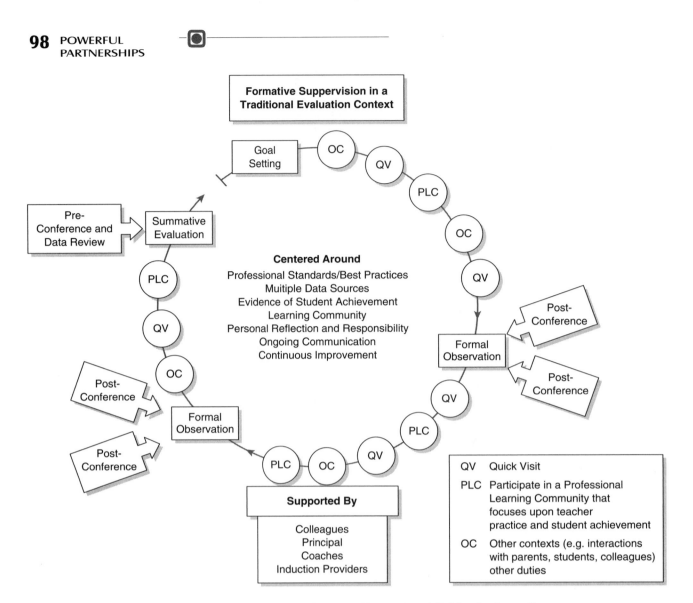

Formative Suppervision in a Traditional Evaluation Context

Centered Around
Professional Standards/Best Practices
Muitiple Data Sources
Evidence of Student Achievement
Learning Community
Personal Reflection and Responsibility
Ongoing Communication
Continuous Improvement

Goal Setting
OC QV PLC OC QV
Pre-Conference and Data Review
Summative Evaluation
PLC QV OC
Post-Conference
Formal Observation
Post-Conference
QV
PLC
Formal Observation
PLC OC QV

Supported By
Colleagues
Principal
Coaches
Induction Providers

QV   Quick Visit

PLC   Participate in a Professional
       Learning Community that
       focuses upon teacher
       practice and student achievement

OC   Other contexts (e.g. interactions
       with parents, students, colleagues)
       other duties

SOURCE: New Teacher Center at University of California, Santa Cruz.

We hope that you spend a significant portion of your time together as a leadership team focusing on teacher supervision. This is the heart of your work, and it should not be done in isolation. Establishing clear expectations of and coaching adult learners (teachers) is not easy, and you will learn from and support one another as you share your challenges. It is also important that you calibrate your observations and expectations with each other. Do you have comparable understandings of what teaching that meets professional standards looks like? Does your leadership team have a shared vision of rigor in instruction, quality student work, and high levels of student engagement?

Discussion Questions

- What specific evidence do you have that teacher supervision is working at your school both in the areas of quality control and professional development?

- What are each of your strength and improvement goals in the area of teacher supervision?

Shared Activities

- Use the *Standards-Based Teaching Practices Worksheet* (modified to match your district's standards) to tease out, in very specific terms, your understandings and expectations in relation to professional standards and practices, and the kinds of evidence, including evidence of learning, that would tie into each standard area you discuss. Once you have had this discussion, visit a series of classrooms and look at actual practice at your school
- Each of you should use the *Teacher Case Studies Worksheet* to identify three teachers you will focus on during the course of this school year. In outlining the history of supervision of each teacher, share the teacher's personnel file and honestly assess the way the process has worked in the past. Discuss your progress in working with these case study teachers on a monthly basis.

Activities for the AP

- If you haven't used the *Teacher Case Studies Worksheet* as a team as described above, use it yourself and discuss your progress with each teacher on a monthly basis with colleagues and/or with your principal.
- Access personnel files at your school and read formative observation and summative evaluation reports. Make your own judgments about what has been done well and what could be improved, and use that knowledge to guide your own work.
- Use the *Formal Observation Protocol Worksheet* to plan and execute a formal observation cycle. Ask your principal or a colleague to observe you in the post-observation conference and to provide you with feedback.

Additional Resources

Danielson, C., & McGreal, T. (2000). *Teacher evaluation: To enhance professional practice.* Alexandria, VA: Association for Supervision and Curriculum Development.

Tools

- Standards-Based Teaching Practices Worksheet
- Teacher Case Studies Worksheet
- Formal Observation Protocol Worksheet

Standards-Based Teaching Practices Worksheet

What do "best practices" look like in each of these areas? Modify to match your own district's adopted professional standards for teaching.			
Standard	**Specific Teacher Behaviors/Practices**	**Specific Student Behaviors and Evidence of Learning**	**Other Evidence/Artifacts of Successful Practice and Learning**
The teacher understands the central concepts, tools of inquiry, and structures of the discipline(s) he or she teaches and can create learning experiences that make these aspects of subject matter meaningful for students.			
The teacher understands and uses a variety of instructional strategies to encourage students' development of critical thinking, problem solving, and performance skills.			
The teacher uses an understanding of individual and group motivation and behavior to create a learning environment that encourages positive social interaction, active engagement in learning, and self-motivation.			
The teacher plans and manages instruction based on knowledge of subject matter, students, the community, and curriculum goals.			
The teacher understands and uses formal and informal assessment strategies to evaluate and ensure the continuous intellectual, social, and physical development of the learner.			

SOURCE: Adapted from Interstate New Teacher Assessment and Support Consortium (INTASC).

Teacher Case Studies Worksheet

Identify an exemplary teacher you supervise who you want to continue to support, an average teacher who can move from "good to great," and a teacher not meeting standards who must either improve or leave. Revisit these case studies with one another on a monthly basis.

	Evidence to Support Your Assessment	Student Achievement Evidence	History of Support and Supervision	Your Goals in Supporting and Supervising This Teacher	Your Plan and Timeline
Exemplary					
Average					
Not Meeting Standards					

Formal Observation Protocol Worksheet

Planning for Formal Observations

Things to Remember

- Your goals are to support teacher growth and development and to ensure that teaching meets professional standards.
- Coaching supports adult learners; use coaching language and listen more than tell.
- Gather evidence before you form opinions. Look for evidence of student engagement and student learning.
- Supervision is a teaching process that should be planned to achieve measurable outcomes.

The Pre-Observation Conference

Things to Determine

- The goals and context of the lesson
- How we will know if the objectives have been met
- Teaching strategies to be employed
- The relation of this observation to earlier formative and summative input
- Focus of the observation, data collection, and relation to professional standards

The Observation

- Use a simple data-collection instrument agreed upon at the pre-conference.
- Gather data on teacher behaviors, student behaviors, and evidence of learning.

The Post-Observation Conference

Before the Conference

- Review the data collected in the context of the teacher's developmental and performance history and evidence of student achievement.
- Determine your desired outcomes for the conference and how you hope to achieve them.

At the Conference

- Ask the teacher to reflect on the lesson; what worked, what didn't, evidence that objectives were met, next steps.
- Share the collected data without judgment; ask the teacher to form his or her own judgments based on the data.
- Share your own judgments, if necessary.
- Tie observations and judgments to professional standards and evidence of student achievement.
- Agree to specific next steps, including timelines.
- Ask the teacher for feedback on the process.

After the Conference

- Reflect on whether or not you successfully used coaching skills and achieved your desired outcomes.
- Follow up with a timely written summary.

CLASSROOM WALKTHROUGHS

The nice thing about Management By Wandering Around is: "What you see is what you get." The . . . BIG IDEA . . . is . . . uh . . . to . . . WANDER AROUND, i.e., stay intimately in touch.

—Tom Peters

Background

There are many reasons why it is critical for school administrators to make frequent unannounced visits to classrooms:

- Classroom walkthroughs provide administrators with important data for the supervision process, which should be formative and ongoing.
- They provide administrators with overall data on schoolwide program issues, providing guidance in program planning, professional development, and a plethora of other areas.
- Feedback to staff based on walkthroughs positively shapes behaviors and culture.
- By being present in classrooms, school leaders communicate their priorities and build relationships and learning community with staff and students.

We want teachers to welcome our presence in classrooms, and we want them to perceive us as valued resources and coaches. We also want teachers to view our principal/assistant principal teams as sharing a focus on instruction and having a common perspective on effective practice. Walkthroughs must be conducted in the spirit of *supporting* effective practice. Unannounced walkthroughs conducted by "inspector generals" reinforce cultures of fear and resentment. Walkthroughs conducted by supportive instructional leaders build professional cultures where open discussion of practice is routine. They provide an opportunity for site leaders to know and be known by students in the single most important context in a school.

The following are suggestions to keep in mind as you plan and conduct these short, informal classroom visitations:

- They should be frequent and unannounced.
- Teachers should receive specific, brief, targeted, positive feedback.
- Data gathered through the process should help you plan professional development, deploy resources, and build relationships with students and staff.
- Team visitations in a variety of configurations, including principal/assistant principal, provide an important vehicle for mentoring, calibration of observations, and shared analysis of school needs. Let teachers know that team observations are part of your own professional development process.

As a leadership team you want your expectations and observations to be "calibrated." That is, you want to share similar visions of quality instruction, and to uphold similar standards of practice. You want to get into classrooms together, so that you can learn from one another. Getting into classrooms in this manner must be among your single highest priorities, if only because it is by influencing what happens in classrooms on the micro level, at the level of teacher-student interactions, that you will shape the success of your school.

A Note on Notes

It is good practice to provide teachers with feedback based on your classroom walkthroughs. We suggest that you do this through short and simple notes. Your feedback should be positive and specific. A statement such as, "Great geometry lesson; students were really into it," does not tell a teacher much about what you are looking for, or the impact of their specific practices. A statement like, "Your movement around the room and interaction with individual students allowed you to monitor independent practice while students used protractors," does.

We suggest that you do not use checklists when doing walkthroughs, as they create an "inspection" sensibility, and they tend to encourage superficial or vague feedback. We have provided a worksheet you and your team might use in gathering data in walkthroughs, and a very simple, sample note format.

You should let teachers know that you will not always write them a note; you may not have much to say . . . or other priorities may come up that make it hard for you to write the note. You don't want teachers to think that if they do not receive a note something is wrong.

If something *is* wrong, if you spot a concern during walkthroughs, you have several options. You can return to the class later to gather more information before drawing conclusions. You can ask the teacher to speak with you during a free period. Where you have a concern of any importance, it is almost always best to have a conversation, rather than to simply leave a note.

There is a corollary benefit to the practice of frequent walkthroughs and what Tom Peters calls "management by wandering around." In the process of getting out into classrooms, you will bump into students and staff and learn about and resolve issues that might have been otherwise invisible to you. You will be more knowledgeable about individual student issues as you conference with parents and staff, and you will nip discipline problems in the bud. Get out there!

Discussion Questions

- How often and effectively have you been conducting walkthroughs up until this point? How can you structure your schedules in order to create more time for effective walkthroughs?
- How will you handle things when you spot a concern during a walkthrough?
- What kind of record keeping should you do around this process?

Shared Activities

- Conduct a series of walkthroughs together and compare your observations, judgments, and thoughts as to next steps in working with teachers.
- Keep copies of your notes to teachers and share them with one another.
- Build a schedule for classroom walkthroughs. Visit some of the same classrooms and compare notes in your weekly meetings.
- Identify a shared focus for your walkthroughs, announce that focus to your staff, and look for opportunities to provide staff with feedback on that focus area. A focus area might include the application of particular teaching strategies, particular content areas, etc.

Activities for the AP

- Make arrangements with a colleague at another school to conduct walkthroughs together at each other's sites.
- Establish a goal of spending a certain percentage of your time in classrooms every week, visiting a certain number of classrooms. Share your goal, and your success in reaching it, with your principal.
- Get into classrooms at a variety of times; what kinds of teaching are going on at the end of the period, in the middle of the morning, in the mid-afternoon?
- During your quick visits, vary your focus; examine student work, watch inter-student interaction, look for evidence of assessment guiding instruction, and interview students.

Tools

- Classroom Walkthrough Record Worksheet
- Sample Walkthrough Note

Classroom Walkthrough Record Worksheet

Date:	Observer:	
Focus of Observations:		
Teacher		
1.	2.	3.
Content		
Teaching Strategies		
Evidence of Learning		
Questions		
Areas for Specific Positive Feedback in Note to Teacher		

Sample Walkthrough Note

Today in your classroom I observed . . .

About 2/3 of your students were able to successfully solve the algebra problems you gave them for guided practice. You circulated in the room and actively coached the students who needed help. You also had posted math vocab. for your English language learners as we had discussed earlier. Glad to see you providing this kind of scaffolding for your students!

Gary

In leaving notes after walkthroughs, *be specific and focus on learning.*

PROFESSIONAL LEARNING COMMUNITIES

Background

Schools are bureaucratic institutions staffed by professionals who often default to working independently and in isolation; what Roland Barth (1990) calls "parallel play." Professional learning communities (PLCs) represent an attempt to break down classroom and office doors to make practice public and to create truly collaborative cultures. Unfortunately, in today's environment a lot of what is being called a PLC is little more than a traditional staff meeting or discussion group.

Etienne Wenger (1998) has been a pioneer in helping organizations establish what he calls Communities of Practice. He states that, "Communities of Practice are formed by people who engage in a process of collective learning in a shared domain of human endeavor: a tribe learning to survive, a band of artists seeking new forms of expression, a group of engineers working on similar problems, a clique of pupils defining their identity in the school, a network of surgeons exploring novel techniques, a gathering of first-time managers helping each other cope." What does a community of practice or PLC look like in a secondary school? It is a math department that meets on a weekly basis to develop common formative and benchmark assessments, analyze student work on those assessments, and strategize to meet the needs of students who are struggling with the exams. It is an English department that recognizes that one of its teachers has more success with low readers than other teachers, and arranges to observe that teacher in action. In an elementary school, it is a grade-level team that meets on a weekly basis to focus on English language acquisition, planning lessons together, sharing student outcome data, observing one another, and sharing direct feedback.

In a review of the research on effective PLCs (Hord, 2005), Southwest Regional Labs identified five key attributes:

1. Collegial and facilitative participation of the principal; shared leadership

2. Unswerving commitment to student learning

3. Collective professional learning applied to practical solutions addressed to student needs

4. Visitation and review of each teacher's classroom behaviors and results by peers with feedback directed at individual and community improvement

5. Physical conditions and human capacities that support such an operation

HOW DO PROFESSIONAL LEARNING COMMUNITIES FALL SHORT?

In our experience in schools around the country, what are being called PLCs are often falling far short of their potential. Following are some of the failures we have observed.

- They never get down to individual teacher's results (in the form of student work, test scores, or observations) and the relation between those results and differences between individual teacher's practices.
- They read and discuss books and articles without implementing ideas and analyzing results.
- Teachers never get into one another's classrooms to gather data and provide feedback.
- They focus on data from annual tests rather than ongoing formative assessments.
- There is no mechanism of accountability to the larger school community.
- Participation is optional (in a true profession, all professionals participate in fundamental processes and practices).

Richard DuFour (1998) suggests that PLCs must engage teachers in examining student work, classroom observation, collaborative inquiry, and coaching for improvement. Key to any PLC process is a focus on student learning in concrete, specific, and personal terms, and a willingness to make individual teaching practice and student progress in individual teacher's classrooms public in a professional setting.

Teacher leadership is essential to any school's PLCs. Your administrative team can work together to identify, train, and empower teacher leaders, and then must get out of the way.

In essence, the principal/assistant principal relationship you are developing if you are working seriously with this book is a small professional learning community and a model for your staff. What follows is a self-assessment you can complete in order to get a read on the level of PLC implementation at your site and suggested activities for both the principal and assistant principal.

Discussion Questions

- Are you participants in a professional learning community? What evidence do you have? How could you strengthen yourselves as a learning community and as a model for others?
- To what extent are your teachers participating in genuine professional communities where they discuss student work, visit one another's classrooms, and share reflections on and feedback about individual practice?

Shared Activities

- Assess the status of learning communities at your site using the *Professional Learning Communities at my Site Worksheet*, and build a plan to strengthen them.

- Identify potential teacher leaders by grade level and/or department. Involve them in the planning and implementation of PLCs at your site, and train them in the basics of meeting facilitation and PLC processes. Design and deliver the training yourselves.

Activities for the AP

- Find an opportunity to participate in job-alike sessions with APs from other sites. Visit each other's schools, observe one another at work, and share direct feedback.
- Over the course of the year, participate in a teacher learning community (a grade-level or department team). Create an opportunity to teach a lesson or series of lessons, and ask for feedback on your teaching from colleagues.

Additional Resources

DuFour, R., & Eaker, R. (1998). *Professional learning communities at work: Best practices for enhancing student achievement.* Bloomington, IN: National Educational Services. Alexandria, VA: Association for Supervision and Curriculum Development.

Hord, S. M. (2004). *Learning together, leading together: Changing schools through professional learning communities.* New York: Teachers College Press.

Tools

- Professional Learning Communities at My Site Worksheet

Professional Learning Communities at My Site Worksheet

Attribute	Where and to What Extent?	Opportunities for Growth
Collegial and facilitative participation of principal; supportive and shared leadership		
Shared values and vision with an unswerving commitment to student learning		
Collective learning and creativity applied to practical solutions addressing student needs		
Shared personal practice characterized by visitation and review of each teacher's classroom behaviors with feedback directed at individual and community improvement		
The time, training, and other resources necessary to make it happen		

SOURCE: Adapted from The Southwest Educational Development Laboratories (SEDL).

USING STUDENT DATA TO IMPROVE TEACHING AND LEARNING

Background

Your ability to collect, analyze, and synthesize student data in ways that inform teaching practice is central to your success as instructional leaders. In schools most focused on improving student learning, teacher data teams regularly collect and discuss student data by student name, use assessment walls to create a visual representation, and hold themselves and each other accountable for improving the learning of all students.

In this day and age, schools are often awash with data, but the data often floats above the classroom, having little or no influence on instruction. Annual summative and norm-referenced tests tell us very little about how to best meet students' needs. More fine-grained assessments, such as quizzes, finals, and analyses of student work, are more likely to be useful to teachers. And data such as teacher-by-teacher failure rates and teacher-by-teacher class attendance may tell us volumes more than annual state assessments. The most valuable summative data are gain scores or value added scores that show student growth from spring to spring or month to month by teacher. You (and your teachers) need to know how students are doing class by class and in comparison to their colleagues.

The effectiveness of school programs and instructional practices should be studied using *a cycle of inquiry*, often called action research. How do we know if a specific literacy program or practice is having a positive affect on student learning? How do we know if our English Language Development program is effective? How do we know if our afterschool tutorial program is having a positive impact? In a cycle of inquiry, one must clearly identify what the problem is that one wants to solve or investigate, the background to this problem, the purpose of the investigation, research questions, the data needed to answer the research questions, and the methods to be used to collect the data.

EVERY SCHOOL LEADER SHOULD HAVE EASY ACCESS TO AND REGULAR USE OF

- *Gain* or *value-added* scores on key academic measures *by teacher* and by student subgroup over time

- Mid-term and semester grade breakdowns *by teacher* and by student subgroup

- Tardies, attendance, detentions, office referals, and suspensions *by teacher* and by student subgroup over time

- Parent, student, graduate, and staff perceptual data about the school and its leadership over time

- Course grade, test score, and retention data for your students promoted to the next level in your system and beyond (e.g., if yours is an elementary school, how do your graduates do in middle school?)

- Graduation and college attendance rates by subgroup

We know that powerful teaching and learning requires skillful, committed teachers and administrators who focus on a limited number of essential learning standards, use a broad diversity of student data to guide teaching and learning on a daily basis, and work with students in a respectful way that holds themselves and every student accountable to master these standards.

One way to organize your work as a leadership team is for each of you to take responsibility for particular departments or grade levels, and to become experts in those areas. As you do so, your challenge is to make connections between data at the most macro level, such as annual state assessments, to data at the micro level, such as student work on a daily assignments, and to teachers' daily practice.

Discussion Questions

- Over the past five years, what evidence do you have of improvement in student achievement at your school? How has data driven and documented that improvement? How have you disaggregated data to target groups and individuals for intervention?
- What data are really being used at your school? How could it be made more accessible and have more of an impact on instruction? What additional data sources could be useful to you and your staff?
- From the student point of view, have you implemented a common curriculum focused on agreed-upon content standards and common formative and summative assessments of learning?

Shared Activities

- On chart paper, map the data sources that are available to you and your teachers and the impacts those data are having on your school and its instructional program. Where are there gaps and opportunities for improvement?
- Use value-added or gain score data to identify an underperforming department, course, or grade level at your school. Parse the data by teacher, subscore, gender, ethnicity, etc. Develop an action plan to engage directly with those teachers through observations, a professional learning community, and targeted professional development.

Activities for the AP

- Identify a comparable school that is producing exceptional student outcomes. Contact the school to determine the types of data being used to inform its initiatives, and the formats and processes that are in place. Share what you find with your leadership team and faculty.
- Work with a target grade-level or department PLC to assess needs, identify power standards, and develop common assessments using the *Power Standards Worksheet* to guide you.

114 POWERFUL
PARTNERSHIPS

- Based on data for a specific subgroup and course, grade level, and/or subject at your school, use the *Action Research Project Format Worksheet* to assess the program's effectiveness and formulate, implement, and evaluate an intervention.

Additional Resources

Sagor, R. (2005). *The action research guidebook: A four-step process for educators and school teams.* Thousand Oaks, CA: Corwin Press.

Schmoker, M. (2004). *The results fieldbook: Practical strategies from dramatically improved schools.* Alexandria, VA: Association for Supervision and Curriculum Development.

Tools

- Power Standards Worksheet
- Action Research Project Format Worksheet

Power Standards Worksheet

Grade Level/Subject/Department/Course:

Participants in the professional learning community engaged in this inquiry:

What are the ten content standards that are most critical for student success in this area?

What do the data tell us, disaggregated by gender, ethnicity, language, teacher, and other relevant factors, about strengths and areas for improvement in relation to these standards to date?

What is our month-by-month curriculum outline/pacing guide with direct reference to the ten power standards?

What common, agreed-upon assessments (such as mid-terms and finals) and benchmark student assignments (such as research projects or labs) should all teachers administer and should we use as common data for analysis in our PLC group?

What subgroups and learning objectives should we target on a month-by-month basis, what interventions should we plan and implement, and how will we evaluate the success of those interventions?

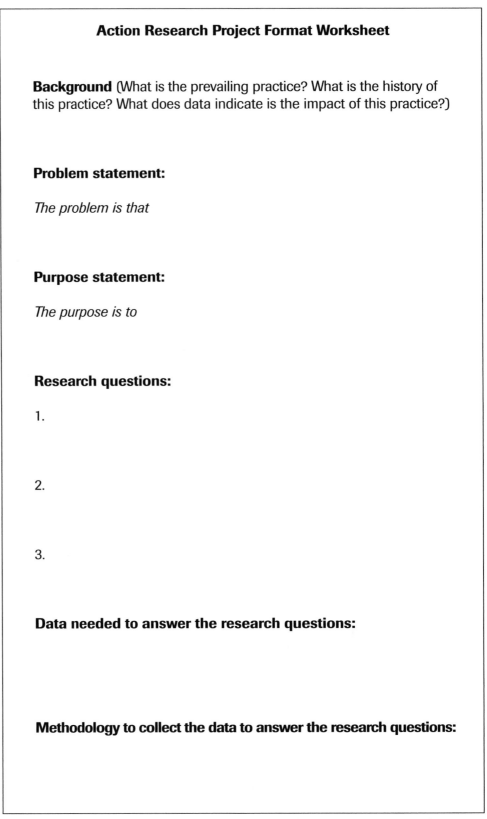

Action Research Project Format Worksheet

Background (What is the prevailing practice? What is the history of this practice? What does data indicate is the impact of this practice?)

Problem statement:

The problem is that

Purpose statement:

The purpose is to

Research questions:

1.

2.

3.

Data needed to answer the research questions:

Methodology to collect the data to answer the research questions:

SCHOOL PLANNING PROCESSES

Background

We're going to assume that your school has a plan or maybe multiple plans. In secondary schools these plans are often tied to accreditation; in most states plans are now required at all levels. We are not, however, going to assume that your plan has a lot to do with daily life in your building. There are plenty of principal/assistant principal teams that go through months without ever referencing their school plans. There are plenty of plans in file cabinets and on shelves that have been produced purely for the purpose of compliance, and that are not serving as the powerful tools they could be.

A school plan is an important tool for instructional leaders. Most of what you have been working on throughout this book should both drive and be driven by your school plan; your vision, your use of staff and resources, and your use of data and professional learning communities. Your decision making should rest on the goals and strategies you have established in your plan. Your plan should outline the ways in which you will evaluate your successes and address your failures.

Principals make two sorts of mistakes in reference to school plans. Some remain hands-off in relation to school plans, communicating that school planning is a compliance activity that doesn't have a whole lot to do with reality at the site. Others keep the planning process close to the vest. Sometimes the goal is to come into compliance in a quick and dirty way. Sometimes the motivation is control. In any of these cases, buy-in is limited and the plan is not likely to have much of an impact.

Outlining an effective school planning process goes beyond the scope of this book. However, we do want to suggest that school plans and the processes that develop them are important to school improvement, and that principals and assistant principals should be out in front in their development and application.

Discussion Questions

- What school plans currently exist? How do they reflect your vision and direction for your school? How often do you and others reference the plans as you make decisions and allocate resources? To what degree are your plans living documents that guide your work, vs. compliance documents you file and forget?

Shared Activities

- When the next accreditation review or plan revision process comes along, collaboratively develop a plan for the process that is data-driven, involves multiple stakeholders, and that will produce a living document that can provide meaningful guidance at your site.

Activities for the AP

- Conduct a case study of a particular portion of your current school plan using the *School Plan Analysis Worksheet*. Share your findings with your leadership team.

Tools

- School Plan Analysis Worksheet

School Plan Analysis Worksheet

School Plan Component:	
Key Goals and Objectives in Plan:	**Key Activities Called for in Plan:**
Evidence of Implementation as Planned:	
Evidence of Successful Outcomes (Data):	
Insights/Comments/Next Steps:	

PROFESSIONAL DEVELOPMENT PLANNING

Background

Professional development occurs on a variety of levels. Powerful professional development occurs at the individual level as you support teachers through the supervision process. Other valuable professional development may be directed at specific groups (novices, a grade level, or department) or at an entire school staff or district. Powerful professional development is consistent with your vision and is determined by your school plan; it is anything but arbitrary. Despite the fact that ongoing quality professional development is one of the most cost-effective investments we can make in schools, most of us have done a poor job in this area. Professional development is often unfocused and unsustained. We fail to apply the very pedagogical standards and practices we expect to see in place in our classrooms. We fail to differentiate, and using a one-size-fits-all model produces disillusionment and cynicism.

Site-based, job-embedded professional development that becomes an integrated part of the daily work within the school best serves the professional growth needs of teachers and thus improves student learning. Effective schools focus on a very limited number of instructional initiatives in any year, and professional learning communities serve as a vehicle for supporting the implementation of those initiatives. Leaders further reinforce those initiatives by focusing on them through formal supervision, walk-throughs, and purposeful daily conversations with staff.

While there may be a role for outside experts as professional development providers at your site, the most effective providers are likely to be you and your teachers. Site-based teacher leaders and content coaches are becoming increasingly important as professional developers.

Assistant principals should have the opportunity to show their stuff as professional development planners and providers. Many APs are coming to the job with stronger backgrounds in curriculum and instruction than the principals they are supporting, and they should not hesitate to bring those strengths to the fore.

Discussion Questions

- How have you provided focused professional development tied to specific student achievement goals this year? To what degree does your PLC and supervision activity support the implementation and evaluation of that professional development focus?

Shared Activities

- Complete the *Professional Development Retrospective Worksheet* together. What insights and action steps can you derive from this exercise?

- Complete the *Professional Development Self-Assessment Worksheet*, based on the National Staff Development Council's standards for staff development together. What insights and action steps can you derive from this exercise?

Activities for the AP

- Work with a target grade-level or department PLC to identify a common professional development focus that is substantiated by student data and aligned with your school plan. Take the lead in identifying internal or external resources for professional development for the group, and in developing, implementing, and monitoring the professional development initiative.
- Design and provide a professional development workshop in an area in which you have expertise for classified or certificated staff. Ask your principal or another colleague to observe and provide you with feedback.

Additional Resources

Speck, M., & Knipe, C. (2001). *Why can't we get it right: Professional development in our schools*. Thousand Oaks, CA: Corwin Press.

National Staff Development Council. Retrieved September 20, 2008, from http://www.nsdc.org/standards/index.cfm

Tools

- Professional Development Retrospective Worksheet
- Professional Development Self-Assessment Worksheet

Professional Development Retrospective Worksheet

Retrospective on Professional Development Outcomes for the Past Two Years			
Teacher	PD Participation	Evidence of Impact on Instruction and Achievement	Possible Needs/Next Steps

Professional Development Self-Assessment Worksheet

At our site, to what degree do we engage in professional development that	Always	Sometimes	Never
Organizes adults into learning communities whose goals are aligned with those of the school and district.			
Provides resources to support adult learning and collaboration.			
Uses disaggregated student data to determine adult learning priorities, monitors progress, and helps sustain continuous improvement.			
Uses multiple sources of information to guide improvement and demonstrate its impact.			
Prepares educators to apply research to decision making.			
Is designed to use appropriate adult learning strategies.			
Is designed to support collaboration and shared ownership.			
Is focused, sustained, and aligned with our school vision and school plan.			
Prepares educators to understand and appreciate all students; creates safe, orderly, and supportive learning environments; and holds high expectations of their academic achievement.			
Deepens educators' content knowledge, provides them with research-based instructional strategies to assist students in meeting rigorous academic standards, and prepares them to use various types of classroom assessments appropriately.			
Provides educators with knowledge and skills to involve families and other stakeholders appropriately.			
Is applied and deepened through the continued focus of learning communities and administrative and teacher leaders.			
Results in teacher cohorts and individual teachers receiving specific feedback regarding the quality of their implementation and its impact upon student achievement.			

SOURCE: Adapted from the National Staff Development Council's Standards for Staff Development.

EPILOGUE

IGNORE THIS PAGE UNTIL JUNE, WHEN THE DUST HAS SETTLED.

Well, congratulations on getting through the school year. In the spirit of continuous improvement and reflective professional practice, we suggest that you not head out the door just yet. We strongly recommend, once the dust has settled, the kids are gone, teachers have checked out, the district is leaving you alone for a change, that as a leadership team you find some quiet, uninterrupted time, perhaps the better part of a day, to discuss the following questions:

- What has worked for you, and what has been problematic for you in your leadership team relationships? Make sure you address:
  - ongoing communication;
  - formal meetings;
  - the utilization of this book and other resources to support your relationship and professional growth;
  - decision making;
  - delegation;
  - sharing responsibilities with the specific intent of developing capacity;
  - maintaining a goals focus; and
  - courageous followership.

- What can you say that you accomplished as a team this year, and what evidence supports that statement?
- How has each of you grown professionally this year, and how as the team contributed to that growth?
- If the principal is hit by a bus this coming September 6, how prepared is the assistant to assume the principalship?
- Based upon your experience this year, what next steps will you commit to
  - in strengthening your leadership team relationship?
  - in directing your personal professional growth and apprentice-ship plan?
  - in exercising effective leadership at your site?

124 OK, you've earned a break! Get out of here!

REFERENCES AND FURTHER READINGS

Ainsworth, L., & Viegut, D. (2006). *Common formative assessments: How to conduce standards-based instruction and assessment.* Alexandria, VA: Association for Supervision and Curriculum Development.

Barth, R. (1990). *Improving schools from within.* San Francisco: Jossey-Bass.

Bloom, G., Warren, B., Castagna, C., & Moir, E. (2005). *Blended coaching: Skills and strategies to support principal development.* Thousand Oaks, CA: Corwin Press.

Bloom, G., et al. (2008). *Leadership institute: Modules for new and other school leaders.* Santa Cruz, CA: The New Teacher Center.

Brinkman, R., & Kraschner, R. (1994). *Dealing with people you can't stand.* New York: McGraw-Hill.

Bryk, A. S., & Schneider, B. L. (2002). *Trust in schools: A core resource for improvement.* New York: Russell Sage Foundation.

Chaleff, I. (1995). *The courageous follower.* San Francisco: Berrett-Koehler.

Collins, J. (2001). *Good to great: Why some companies make the leap . . . and others don't.* New York: HarperBusiness.

Covey, S. R. (1996). *First things first.* New York: Fireside.

Danielson, C., & McGreal, T. (2000). Teacher evaluation to enhance professional practice. Alexandria, VA: Association for Supervision and Curriculum Development.

Daresh, J. (2001). *Leaders helping leaders.* Thousand Oaks, CA: Corwin Press.

Deal, T., & Peterson, K. (1999). *Shaping school culture: The heart of leadership.* San Francisco: Jossey-Bass.

De Waal, F. (2001). *The ape and the sushi master: Cultural reflections by a primatologist.* New York: Perseus Books.

DuFour, R., & Eaker, R. (1998). *Professional learning communities at work: Best practices for enhancing student achievement.* Bloomington: IN: National Educational Services. Alexandria, VA: Association for Supervision and Curriculum Development.

Heider, J. (1985). *The tao of leadership.* Lake Worth, FL: Humanics Publishing Group.

Hord, S. M. (2004). *Learning together, leading together: Changing schools through professional learning communities.* New York: Teachers College Press.

ISLLC. (2008). *Standards.* Washington, DC: Council of Chief State School Officers. Retrieved August 10, 2008, from http://www.ccsso.org/projects/Interstate_Consortium_on_School_Leadership/ISLLC_Standards/

Kouzes, J., & Pozner, B. (1992). *The leadership challenge.* San Francisco: Jossey-Bass.

Krovetz, M. (2008). *Fostering resilience: Expecting all students to use their minds and hearts well.* Thousand Oaks, CA: Corwin Press.

Krovetz, M., & Arriaza, G. (2006). *Collaborative teacher leadership: How teachers can foster equitable schools.* Thousand Oaks, CA: Corwin Press.

Lambert, L. (2003). *Leadership capacity for lasting school improvement.* Alexandria, VA: Association for Supervision and Curriculum Development.

Lencioni, P. (2004). *Death by meeting.* San Francisco: Jossey-Bass.

Lindstrom, P., & Speck, M. (2004). *The principal as professional development leader.* Thousand Oaks, CA: Corwin Press.

Marzano, R. (2003). *What works in schools: Translating research into action.* Alexandria, VA: Association for Supervision and Curriculum Development.

Marzano, R. I., Waters, T., & McNulty, B. (2005). *School leadership that works: From research to results.* Alexandria, VA: Association for Supervision and Curriculum Development.

McDonald, J. (2007). *The power of protocols: An educator's guide to better practice.* New York: Teachers College Press.

Milius, S. (2005, August 20). Getting the gull: Baiting trick spreads among killer whales. *Science News,* 118.

Morley, C. (1994). *How to get the most out of meetings.* Alexandria VA: Association for Supervision and Curriculum Development.

National School Public Relations Association, http://nspra.org

National Staff Development Council. Retrieved September 20, 2008, from http://www.nsdc.org/standards/index.cfm

Northwest Regional Educational Laboratory. (2001).*The power of public relations in schools.* Retrieved September 20, 2008, from http://www.nwrel.org/request/feb01/

Neubig, M. (2007). *The practitioners guide to scheduling for SLCs and career academies: Equity in action.* Carlsbad, CA: Hudson Publishing.

Ohle, N., & Morley, C. (1994). *How to solve typical school problems.* Alexandria, VA: Association for Supervision and Curriculum Development.

Peters, T., & Waterman, R. (2004). *In search of excellence.* New York: HarperCollins.

Peterson, K. (1994). *Building collaborative cultures: Seeking ways to reshape urban schools.* Naperville, IL: North Central Regional Educational Laboratory.

Peterson, K. (1995). *Building a collective vision.* Naperville, IL: North Central Regional Educational Laboratory. Retrieved August 17, 2008, from http://www.ncrel.org/sdrs/areas/issues/educatrs/leadrshp/le100.htm

Sagor, R. (2005). *The action research guidebook: A four-step process for educators and school teams.* Thousand Oaks, CA: Corwin Press.

Saphier, T., & Pierson, G. (1989). *How to make decisions that stay made.* Carlisle, MA: Research for Better Teaching.

Schmoker, M. (2004). *The results fieldbook: Practical strategies from dramatically improved schools.* Alexandria, VA: Association for Supervision and Curriculum Development.

Speck, M., & Knipe, C. (2001). *Why can't we get it right: Professional development in our schools.* Thousand Oaks, CA: Corwin Press.

Spillane, J. P., Halverson, R., & Diamond, J. B. (2001, April). Investigating school leadership practice: A distributed approach. *Educational Researcher, 30*(3) 23–28.

Wenger, E. (1998). *Communities of practice: Learning, meaning, and identity.* Cambridge, UK; New York: Cambridge University Press.

Zachary, L. (2005). *Creating a mentoring culture.* San Francisco: Joseey-Bass.

INDEX

CORWIN PRESS

The Corwin Press logo—a raven striding across an open book—represents the union of courage and learning. Corwin Press is committed to improving education for all learners by publishing books and other professional development resources for those serving the field of PreK–12 education. By providing practical, hands-on materials, Corwin Press continues to carry out the promise of its motto: **"Helping Educators Do Their Work Better."**